P9-BUH-252

FATHERS
LIVING A LIFE OF LEADERSHIP...
GOD'S WAY

WHITE STONE BOOKS
LAKELAND, FLORIDA

07 06 05 04 03   10 9 8 7 6 5 4 3 2 1

FATHERS—LIVING A LIFE OF LEADERSHIP...GOD'S WAY
ISBN 1-59379-007-4
COPYRIGHT © 2003 JOHN M. THURBER
THURBER CREATIVE SERVICES, INC.
TULSA, OKLAHOMA

EDITORIAL DEVELOPMENT AND LITERARY REPRESENTATION BY
MARK GILROY COMMUNICATIONS, INC.
6528 E. 101ST STREET, SUITE 416
TULSA, OKLAHOMA 74133-6754

EDITORIAL MANAGER: CHRISTY STERNER

PUBLISHED BY WHITE STONE BOOKS, INC.
P.O. BOX 2835
LAKELAND, FLORIDA 33806

*I*NTRODUCTION

He has made His wonderful works to be remembered.
PSALM 111:4 NKJV

God is faithfully at work today in the lives of people around the world—revealing His ways, demonstrating His power, and expressing His infinite love. Do you know that He wants to do the same for you?

Are you looking for answers to the many questions you deal with as a father?

Do you seek wisdom on practicing the consistent leadership and discipline you want to provide for your children?

Perhaps you are face-to-face with pressures regarding your career or need insight in dealing with a challenging situation in your home. Are you looking for answers on how to balance the demands of your career and the needs of your family?

God's Way for Fathers is filled with true stories that present powerful, spiritual insights from men experiencing the same range of life situations you face; from fathers who have looked to God for wisdom and encouragement—and received it.

Prepare to encounter new levels of power and excellence in your life as you seek to achieve and determine to discover what it truly means to live a life of leadership...*God's Way.*

Contents

THE PARADOX OF POWER ❧ *Charles Colson* 11

ONE SUMMER DAY ❧ *Jay Cookingham* 15

THE DAY THE CHEERING STOPPED
     ❧ *John C. Stewart, as told to Gloria Cassity Stargel* ..19

A PLACE CALLED FORGIVENESS ❧ *Bradley S. Collins* 25

HOW TO MAKE A MOOSE RUN ❧ *Gary Stanley*........................29

THE NAIL ❧ *Max Davis* 33

EXCUSE ME SIR, IS YOUR DAUGHTER IN TROUBLE?
     ❧ *Charles Stanton* 39

THE NEW FATHER FOG ❧ *Michael T. Powers* 43

A FATHER'S PRIDE AND JOY ❧ *David Flanagan*........................49

POSTCARDS FROM MY SON ❧ *Charlie "Tremendous" Jones* 53

A VERY LUCKY MAN
     ❧ *Roy C. Gibbs, as told to Nancy B. Gibbs*...................57

THE STRANGE ROAD TO SUCCESS ❧ *Joe Gibbs* 61

A PROMISE KEPT ❧ *Kristi Powers* 65

SWIMMING ON DADDY'S BACK ❧ *Gary Stanley*........................69

THE GOAL OF MY LIFE ❧ *Paul Henderson* 73

DAD'S "COAT OF MANY HORRORS" ❧ *Todd and Jedd Hafer* 77

WINNING ISN'T ENOUGH ❧ *Tom Lehman* 81

GOD TOOK ME IN ❧ *Ken Freeman* 85

WINNING WAYS ❧ *Michael Chang* 95

REDEFINING SUCCESS ❧ *Ed Becker* 99

WITHOUT FEAR ❧ *Roger Neilson*..103

PINTO BEANS AND FRIED BOLOGNA—NOW THAT'S A FEAST OF FAITH
     ❧ *Stan Toler* 107

FREED FROM RELIGION ❧ *Billy Diamond*..113

NO TIME TO LIVE
     ❧ *Joe H. Stargel, with Gloria Cassity Stargel* 117

LIKE A ROCK ❧ *Jay Cookingham* 123

HEAVEN'S REWARDS ❧ *Nancy B. Gibbs* 127

THANKS FOR HAVING ME!
    ❧ *Jerry Wayne Bernard, as told to Muriel Larson* 131

FIRMLY PLANTED ❧ *Tripp Curtis* 137

FROM GRIEF TO GIFTS ❧ *Joe Tye* 143

HOME FOR CHRISTMAS
    ❧ *Richard C. Stargel, with Gloria Cassity Stargel* ..149

THE BANNER OF LOVE ❧ *Nancy Gibbs* 157

LOCKING UP FOR THE NIGHT ❧ *Robin Bayne* 161

THE THIRD MIRACLE ❧ *Liana Metal* 165

ON BENDED KNEE ❧ *Carol Termin* 171

WINNERS AND LOSERS ❧ *David Flanagan* 173

I FOUND HOPE ❧ *Kevin Whitworth* 177

OKAY, GOD, IF YOU'RE LISTENING, WHY AREN'T YOU ANSWERING?
    ❧ *Stan Toler* 183

A BRIGHT FUTURE ❧ *Clarence Smith* 189

THE OLD MAN ❧ *Ruben Tijerina* 197

KEEP YOUR EYE ON THE BALL ❧ *Michael Dirmeier* 201

ARMS WIDE OPEN ❧ *Emilio Castillo* 207

WAIT FOR ME, DADDY ❧ *Byard Hill* 213

WHISTLIN' WILLIE ❧ *Pat Middleton* 219

WHEN I WAS A PRODIGAL SON ❧ *Don Hall* 227

DAD WOULDN'T SAY ❧ *John Ashcroft* 233

THE EVERYDAY, STREET-WALKIN', DOOR-BANGIN' SALESMAN
    ❧ 237

RIGHTS AND PERMISSIONS 247

MEET THE CONTRIBUTORS 251

TELL US YOUR STORY 255

FATHERS
LIVING A LIFE OF LEADERSHIP...
GOD'S
WAY

$\mathcal{T}$HE PARADOX OF POWER

CHARLES COLSON

Whosoever will save his life will lose it: and whosoever

will lose his life for my sake shall find it.

MATTHEW 16:25

When I was thirty-nine, the president of the United States asked me to serve as his special counsel. It was one of the most powerful positions in the world. Every day, National Security Advisor Henry Kissinger walked into our briefing sessions with a worried, dour look on this face and said, "The decision we are going to make today will change the future course of human history." He said that five days a week, fifty-two weeks a year.

Looking back, I realize we didn't change anything. Oh sure, we dealt with Congress, or the newspapers, but we didn't change how people really lived. It was in prison, where I served time for my involvement in the Watergate conspiracy, that I learned about real power.

I certainly knew nothing of it in my early days. I grew up watching people wait in bread lines, all the while telling myself, *The most important thing is for me to go to college.* As it turned out, I won a scholarship to Brown University and graduated with honors. During the Korean War, I was commissioned as a lieutenant in the Marines. The war ended, and I earned a doctorate in law and started a successful law firm. Soon, I was involved in politics, becoming the youngest administrative assistant in the United States Senate. Next step: the White House with President Richard Nixon. Limousines waited for me. Admirals and generals saluted. I had everything a person could want. Curiously enough, that was the first time I felt empty inside.

As the Watergate scandal unfolded, one friend in particular was a source of encouragement. But he had changed since I'd seen him last, and I asked him why he was different. He looked me straight in the eye and said, "I accepted Jesus Christ and committed my life to Him." I took a firm grip on the bottom of my chair. I thought just little old ladies standing on street corners talked like that. But here was a practical businessman, an engineer, talking about Jesus Christ as if He were here today. I nervously changed the subject. But I visited him again a few months later and asked him to tell me more.

He told me how he, too, had started out with nothing and

had risen to a position of power, but felt empty. He began a search for God that ended in a seat at Madison Square Garden, listening to Billy Graham speak about Jesus Christ. He did not describe Him as an ancient historical figure but as a living God who rose from the dead and lives today.

My friend wanted me to pray with him that night, but I didn't. I was too proud. I was known as the toughest of Nixon's tough guys, the White House "hatchet man." But that night I couldn't get my car out of my friend's driveway because I was crying too hard. I wanted more than anything to be at peace with God. *Just take me, God,* I cried. *Take me the way I am.* The next morning, I felt a wonderful peace.

As the Watergate scandal unfolded and I went to prison, I learned—to my surprise—just where the true power in life really is. It was in a little prayer group where two dope pushers, a car thief, a stock swindler, and a former special counsel for the president of the United States got down on our knees at night and prayed. We saw men give their lives to Christ, their hearts transformed by the power of the living God.

Why Jesus and not some other religious leader? The truth turns on the fact of Jesus Christ's bodily resurrection from the dead. I know the resurrection is a fact, and Watergate proved it to me. How? Because twelve men testified that they had seen Jesus raised from the dead, and then they proclaimed that truth for forty years, never once denying it. Every one of them was beaten, tortured, stoned, or put in prison. They would not have endured all of that suffering if what they believed wasn't true.

Watergate embroiled twelve of the most powerful men in the world—and they couldn't keep a lie for three weeks. You're telling me the twelve apostles could keep a lie for forty years? Absolutely impossible.

Today, I thank God for Watergate. It taught me the greatest lesson of my life, the paradox of power: that he who seeks to save his life will lose it, but he who loses his life for the sake of Christ shall find it.

ONE SUMMER DAY

JAY COOKINGHAM

Carry each other's burdens, and in this way you will fulfill the law of Christ.

GALATIANS 6:2 NIV

His name is Jack, and all summer he has tried to swim to the small floating dock positioned in the deep part of the local swimming hole. Jack's a good swimmer, but he doesn't have the confidence that he can make it all the way out there. Every time he's tried he has given up about halfway and gone back to shallow water. It's a hot summer day, and today Jack wants to try again, but he's still unsure and hesitant to start. However, all this is about to change.

Two brothers come to the park with their family, jump into the lake, and swim up to Jack. Within minutes they are all fast friends, and the brothers encourage Jack that he can make it to the float, and just to make sure, they will swim alongside him. When the three of them make it to the float, there is a riotous celebration of the triumphant swim—Jack has finally achieved his goal! They all swim back to tell their moms of the great victory and the mighty swim, excitedly retelling the details, all talking at once and all beaming with pride.

Three boys, one pond, and maybe a turning point in all of their lives. The two boys were my older sons, Josh and Matt, and they stepped (or should I say, dove) into a major "blessing moment." They came alongside someone and made a difference in that person's life.

In my teens, I backslid away from God's way for a few years, and I went through a difficult transition when I returned to the fold. The "float" for me was the acceptance by the people of my church. At the time, I wanted to swim there, but I wasn't sure I could make it. Then a brother came up beside me and he helped me make that move by simply becoming my friend. He didn't realize then (nor did I) the huge impact that would make on my life. He is my best friend to this day.

There are times when we need a brother to come alongside us and help us get to a place we need to be, a place we might not make it to on our own. Jack allowed my two sons to help him through his trial by water—he was trusting that his new friends would not let him down.

My sons were able to put into practice what I have been able to model for them by God's grace—and what was modeled for me in my own Christian walk.

Galatians 6:2 says to "carry each other's burdens, and in this way you will fulfill the law of Christ." The impact that we have when we do this—the ripples on the pond of life—are far reaching when we honor Christ in this way.

THE DAY THE CHEERING STOPPED

JOHN C. STEWART

(As told to Gloria Cassity Stargel; names in this story have been changed)

There is rejoicing in the presence of the angels

of God over one sinner who repents.

LUKE 15:10 NIV

It happened on a cold day in January, midway through my senior year in high school. I tossed my books into the locker and reached for my black and gold Cougar jacket. From down the corridor, a friend called out, "Good luck, Johnny. I hope you get the school you want!"

Playing football was more than a game to me. It was my *life*. So the world looked pretty wonderful as I headed up the hill toward the gym to learn which college wanted me on their team.

How I counted on the resulting scholarship—I had for years! It held my only hope for higher education. My dad, an alcoholic, had left home long ago, and Mom worked two jobs just to keep seven children fed. I held down part-time jobs to help out.

But I wasn't worried. I had the grades I needed. And ever since grammar school, I had lived and breathed football. It was my entire identity.

Growing up in a little southern town where football is king, my skills on the field made me a big man in the community as well as on my high-school campus. I pictured myself right up there on a pedestal—where most people would place me.

Everyone helped to pump up my ego. The local newspaper mentioned me in write-ups; at football games exuberant cheerleaders yelled out my name; people constantly made comments like, "You can do it, Johnny. You can go all the way to professional football!" That was heady stuff and I ate it up. In a way, it made up for my not having a dad to encourage me along the way.

Hurrying to the gym that day, I recalled all those football games—and all those *injuries!* I never had let any of them slow me down for long—not the broken back or the messed up shoulders and knees—I just gritted my teeth and played right through the agony. I *had* to.

And now came the reward. A good future would be worth the price I had paid. So with a confident grin on my face, I sauntered into Coach Stone's office.

Coach sat behind his desk, the papers from my file spread before him. Our three other coaches sat around the room. No doubt about it, this lineup signaled a momentous occasion.

"Have a seat, Johnny," Coach motioned to the chair beside his desk.

"Johnny," he started, "you've worked really hard. You've done a good job for us. A couple of colleges want to make you an offer."

Something about his tone made me nervous. I shifted my sitting position.

"But, Johnny," he said, holding my medical records in his hands, "Doctor Kendley can't recommend you for college football. Johnny, one more bad hit, and you could be paralyzed for life. We can't risk it."

A long silence followed. Then Coach Stone's eyes met mine. "I'm sorry, Johnny. There will be no scholarship."

No scholarship?! The blow hit me like a 300-pound linebacker slamming against my chest. Somehow I got out of that office. I could not seem to understand that they were thinking of my best welfare. Instead, all I could think was, *You're not good enough, you're not good enough, you're not good enough.*

For *me*, the cheering stopped. Without the cheering, I was

nothing. And without college, I would *stay* a nothing.

After that, I just gave up. And in so doing, I lost my grip on life.

At first, I settled for beer and marijuana. Soon I got into the hard stuff: acid, PCP, heroin, cocaine—I tried them all. By the time graduation rolled around, I wonder how I even made it through the ceremonies.

Several older friends tried to talk to me about God. Yet even though I had grown up in church, I couldn't grasp the fact that God had anything to do with my present situation.

A couple of buddies and I decided to hit the road. We had no money and no goal. Along the way, we got into stealing gas to keep us going. When we got hungry enough, we picked up some odd jobs. No matter how little food we had, we always managed to get more drugs.

My anger continued to build. It wasn't long until I got into a bad fight and landed in jail thousands of miles from home. It caused me to take a good look at myself and see how low I had sunk. *God,* I prayed for the first time in years, *please help me. I'm lost, and I can't find my way back.*

I didn't hear an immediate answer. Nor did I clean up my act. We *did* head toward home, but the old car had had enough. It quit.

I went into a garage, hoping to get some cheap parts. *Maybe*

I can patch her up enough to get us home. I was tired, hungry, dirty—and very much under the influence. Yet a man there extended a hand of friendship. He even took us to supper. After we were fed, Mr. Brown called me aside, "Son," he said, "you don't have to live like this. You can be somebody if only you'll try. God will help you. Remember, He loves you. And so do I."

I was buffaloed. He seemed to care about me. And he had called me "son." It had been a long, long time since a man had called me "son."

That night, in my sleeping bag, I gazed up at the star-filled Texas night. The sky looked so close, I thought maybe I could reach up and touch it. And once again, I tried to pray. *Lord, I am so tired. If You'll have me, I'm ready to come back to You.*

In my heart, I heard God answer, *I'm here. Come on back, son. I'm here.* He called me "son," just like Mr. Brown did. I liked that.

On the road again, I got to thinking: *If Mr. Brown, a complete stranger, thinks I can make something of myself, maybe I can.*

I didn't straighten out all at once. But at least I started trying. And God kept sending people to help me. Like Susan. In September, this cute young thing—a casual friend from high school—came up to me at a football game, of all places. She kissed me on the cheek, and said, "Welcome home, Johnny."

The day she said, "Johnny, if you keep doing drugs, I can't date you anymore," was the day I quit them for good.

Susan and I married and today we have three beautiful children. We're active in our local church and operate a successful business. I can tell you it means the world to me to have earned the respect of my community.

All these years later, I still can feel the sting of that day—the day the cheering stopped. The hurt doesn't linger though, as I've learned I can live without the cheers of a human crowd. After all, I have a caring Heavenly Father who calls me "son." And I do have a cheering section—a Heavenly one. Check out this Bible verse I discovered: "There is rejoicing in the presence of the angels of God over one sinner who repents" (Luke 15:10 NIV).

How about that?

Angels! Cheering for ME!

I like that.

A PLACE CALLED FORGIVENESS

BRADLEY S. COLLINS

...His compassions fail not. They are new every morning...

LAMENTATIONS 3:22-23

"Daddy, when you do something bad and ask God to forgive you, do you still go to hell?"

As we sat in the parking lot of the Wal-Mart Supercenter that Sunday afternoon, Whitney's face exhibited the pained evidence of torment, so I asked, "Did you ask God to forgive you for something?" She replied, "Yes." Well," I offered, "do you still feel like you're in hell?" "Yes," was again her answer.

Earlier in the day, reprisal of a behavior that my then ten-year-old daughter had begun to display more frequently had broken through. For unknown reasons at the time, Whitney would dig her heels in when she was upset and absolutely refuse to relent. Words like "I hate you!" "You don't love me!"

and "You never do anything for me!" were becoming commonplace when my historically sweet, loving, polite child began to back herself into an emotional corner. Making the unpleasant interactions even less understandable was the open, loving, and communicative relationship Whitney and I had enjoyed in the past.

Assorted friends and relatives had attempted to appease me by writing the outbursts off as "just a phase" or a "stage" she was going through, but I truly believed I knew my daughter better than that. I also sensed that, just as confident as I was about Whitney's experiencing some sort of internal agony, I was very sure that, in her own time, she would find the motivation to talk about her troubles. I couldn't force the issue and expect her to freely open up about it.

Sundays were typically tough for us anyway because that meant that it would be time, in a few short hours, to return Whitney to her mom's home. Her mom and I had been divorced for several years, and while school was in session, 6:30 P.M. Sunday evening was the standard departure time, the ending to our weekend together. Yes, Sundays were always difficult but this particular Sunday felt profoundly tense.

Whitney had wanted me to pick up one of her friends and bring her over to play. For a reason which presently escapes me, I found it necessary to say "no." The verbal onslaught began. As I bit my own lip to avoid retaliation or another ineffective punitive response, Whitney decided to take the barrage up a notch, threatening to refuse to leave the house to accompany me on a shopping journey that we'd been planning for a while.

"You go. I'm staying here." "I'm not going anywhere with you!" "You don't love me!" Her obvious pain was shooting right through me.

Before long, I had convinced Whit that not only was she not old enough to stay home by herself, but the possibility of losing more of her freedom and privileges was about to become a reality.

She departed in a huff, wearing a scowl for about the first forty-five minutes of the shopping trip, not uttering a word. I made unreciprocated small talk in intervals, for no other reason than to make Whitney aware that I would be ready when she was.

When we pulled into the Wal-Mart parking lot, I said, "Whit, you're not going to run me off. I'm your dad. I will always be your dad. I will always love you."

That's when she swallowed her pride and made her inquiry about God and His forgiveness.

"Honey, maybe the reason that you still feel the way you do about it is because sometimes God needs our help. Sometimes we have to forgive ourselves before we can feel better about something we've done. I can only tell you that sharing things I have felt guilty about with someone I trust has helped me to get past many of the regrets that haunted me. It allowed me to forgive myself and accept the fact that I'm not perfect."

Whitney broke down, cried long and hard, and through her tears, entrusted me with the knowledge of a deed so big and ugly to her that it had affected her relationships for several months.

Naturally, the act Whitney confessed to me—and over which she had bludgeoned herself, for what, I am certain felt like an eternity to her—was a minor transgression, except for the toll it took upon her.

Just as powerful was the immediate benefit of sharing her trouble. As evidenced by her ability to talk openly about real life issues since that day, Whitney experienced a release from the burden of carried guilt. She understands that many times in life we are only as sick as our secrets.

The relief that my daughter received was evident then and remains so, even to this day. She is now fourteen-and-a-half (don't forget the "half!") and, to my knowledge Whitney has never had that attitude of unforgiveness toward herself again. She has learned that it is easier for God to do His job when we do ours.

$\mathcal{H}$OW TO MAKE A MOOSE RUN

GARY STANLEY

Listen, my sons, to a father's instruction;

pay attention and gain understanding.

PROVERBS 4:1 NIV

Unless you're actually trying to carry a tune, I figure a good whistle is only about one thing—volume—an earsplitting, glass-breaking, through-the-teeth, taxi-alerting loud sort of whistle. I've had a dozen gifted whistlers attempt to teach me how to make this shrill noise, but they've all failed. It still remains one of life's great mysteries to me.

Not possessing this kind of whistle has been a severe handicap in my audible range of expression, but I've learned to adapt with a modicum of grace and civility. (But I do still think it's cruelly unfair that some can, and I can't!) However, I can whistle at a "normal" volume. In fact, I even know four ways of doing so. Dad taught me three, and the other one I picked up from my longtime buddy, Mike.

I can pucker my lips and whistle both out and in. (That's two ways.) Mike taught me to roll my tongue lengthwise and blow across it much the way you do a pop bottle to get a foghorn sound—took me years to perfect that one. But the fourth way is my dad's patented "moose call." It uses both hands placed together to make an air pocket so that your two thumbs can bend to cover the only opening. It's important that there be just one opening and no leaks or else it won't work— trust me. Then you put your upper lip over both bent thumb knuckles and blow straight down. If you're really good, you can slightly open one hand and get a two-pitch sound reminiscent of a tugboat whistle.

Dad and I called moose all the time from our front yard, at football games, on camping trips, and any other place where a good stout whistle was appropriate. And we never saw a single moose for all that blowing.

Then the summer of my eighth year, we took a family vacation to Yellowstone National Park—we experienced Old Faithful, a massive visitors' lodge made of giant timbers and crossbeams, begging bears aplenty, my first earthquake…and a herd of moose!

A dozen moose were grazing in a meadow about a hundred

yards back from the road. Between the moose and us was a seven- or eight-foot-high barbed wire fence. It was one of those no-nonsense fences strung tight with vertical wire woven between the horizontal strands to keep them together.

Dad pulled the car over, and I jumped out ready to test our moose call. I positioned my hands just right and blew long and clear—even added the two-pitched trick for good measure. Not one of the moose moved. Didn't even look up between chews.

Dad put his arm around me and said, "Maybe they won't come when we call, but I bet we could make those moose run! Wanna try?" With that, he started to work his way over the barbed-wire fence. I squeezed between the bottom two wires. That fence was strung so tight there wasn't any give in it at all. It took us the better part of five minutes to get across without getting cut, stuck, or poked.

Once on the other side, we started to walk toward the herd. Dad waved his arms and hollered, and I continued to work my moose call. We marched forward like a couple of crazy tourists. The herd of moose continued to ignore us in favor of munching the meadow. They'd probably seen it all before. We continued forward, waving, hollering, and whistling.

Then Dad picked up a pebble and flipped it in the general direction of the moose. That got their attention. The biggest moose in the herd finally looked up. He had a massive set of antlers and looked to be nearly seven feet tall. Probably tipped the scales at more than a thousand pounds. He picked up hooves the size of hubcaps and began to move. It was an amazing thing to watch—all that bulk picking up steam. It was all the more fascinating because he was moving in our direction! Still a good eighty yards from us, he was already too close for comfort!

"Run!" Dad hollered.

We put on a good show for the moose as we turned tail and scrambled for the fence. I suspect we turned in several personal bests that day—a new record for the twenty-yard dash, Dad's two-step fence climb, and my belly-flop wiggle under the wire. It's amazing what you can do when an angry moose is involved.

We caught our breath, hugged Mom, and got back in the car. For the next twenty miles, our conversation bounced back and forth between our foolishness, a growing respect for God's larger creatures, and our own miraculous escape. A few miles down the road, it occurred to Dad that we undoubtedly possessed the best moose call in the world: one that doesn't work!

Wisdom knows when to abandon one plan in favor of a better one.

$\mathcal{T}$HE NAIL

MAX DAVIS

The Lord is close to those whose hearts are breaking.

PSALM 34:18 TLB

On my daughter Kristen's tenth birthday, the unimaginable happened. We were celebrating a normal birthday party. What could go wrong at a child's birthday party, right?

Some relatives had helped decorate. As a part of the decorations, they'd hung balloons all around the front porch. They were hung on nails that had been driven securely into the wood to hang potted plants. One of the balloons was the thick latex type, with a heavy-duty rubber band attached—the kind that you bounce back and forth off your knuckles while holding the rubber band.

As the scenario unfolded, my son, James, wanted a balloon—not just any balloon, but "*that* balloon." It was within his reach, so he grabbed it and did what any eight-year-old would do. He started pulling. But the rubber band was attached to the nail and wouldn't come down. The more James pulled, the tighter the rubber band stretched. Then, in a microsecond, the nail, not the balloon, was dislodged. The force of the stretched rubber band bulleted the nail directly into James' chest, embedding it there. You can imagine our shock as James came stumbling into the living room, stunned, with a three-inch nail driven into his chest!

It was not a pretty sight. The nail had projected through his bone and was driven so deep that we thought he might die. We were scared to move him because we didn't know if the nail had hit an artery or a lung or what. Someone called 911. Soon an ambulance and fire truck filled our front lawn. Lights were flashing everywhere. Cars were slowing down on the street to inquire. Kristen's birthday cake and presents lay untouched as the paramedics worked intensely. The girls were crying. The paramedics secured James so he could not move, slid him into the ambulance, and whisked him away as my father-in-law and I followed. They would not allow me to ride in the ambulance with my own son. James watched in terror, screaming for me to come, but all I could do was watch.

You see, my son is totally deaf. What must have gone through his mind during that ambulance ride? *Why has Daddy left me? Why won't he come?*

At the hospital, the x-rays revealed that the nail had barely missed an artery and was resting on his lung. Mercifully, it had not punctured it. The ER doctor's words went like this: "It is evident that Someone upstairs is watching over your son, because if that nail had lodged a half-inch in either direction, he would be dead. Or the nail could have hit his eye or gone into his head." Then the doctor told me, "We could put him under anesthesia and do surgery to remove the nail, but for someone as young as James, that might cause further complications. We need to get the nail out now." Then he looked at me and said, "It's going to be painful. But it's for the best."

James was given pain medication, but it had little effect and he was screaming. The doctor instructed me to hold my son down while he attempted to remove the nail. Soon we realized that this was going to be a much more difficult task than we had first thought.

Each time the doctor merely touched the nail, the pain would send James jerking and screaming. The doctor took a pair of pliers and started pulling the nail, but it wouldn't budge. It was driven in his chest like a nail hammered into a piece of lumber. Because of his deafness, James couldn't talk, but the whole time his eyes were locked onto mine. They pierced through me and said it all: "Daddy, do something. Don't let the doctor hurt me. Please, Daddy, please." I too was in tears and, in a moment of weakness, I let go.

The doctor sternly confronted me and said I had to be strong and hold him down. "It is for James' own good," he reminded me again. Despite knowing what was best, holding my son down was one of the hardest things I've ever had to do. I also knew that I had within me the authority to stop the whole procedure and request surgery. My instincts as a father, however, told me that this was the best thing to do in the long run. So, I took a deep breath and, once again, wrapped my arms around James and held him down—this time more tightly than before. The whole time his eyes never stopped speaking to me: "Dad, how could you betray me, you of all people? I trusted you. You know how this is hurting me. Daddy, I'm in pain. Do something!"

Yet, all I could do was hold him down. This time, the doctor literally straddled James and pulled with his arms using his legs for more power. That's how deeply lodged the nail was. Finally, after what seemed an eternity, the nail popped out. James and I sat there, in a pile of sweat, exhausted and emotionally spent. The pain subsided. The distress was over. James looked at me, as if to say "Daddy, why did you let them do that to me?" All I could do was hold him in my arms and love him. He couldn't understand why I had done what I did, and words wouldn't matter. *When he gets older and more mature,* I thought, *then he will understand.*

Only another parent can know the torment I was going through. And yet as I think of how much I love my son and was hurting for him—I am reminded and greatly moved by God's love for us. So profound is His love that He gave His only Son, so we could have eternal life.

Excuse me, sir, is your daughter in trouble?

CHARLES STANTON

Pray that I'll know what to say and have the

courage to say it at the right time.

EPHESIANS 6:19 THE MESSAGE

I am not normally one of those people who says, "God spoke to me and told me to tell you something." But one time I had an experience I can't explain any other way. I was seated between two large businessmen on a jam-packed airplane. I pulled out my handy-dandy inflatable neck pillow and scrunched down for a little nap, but I couldn't sleep. Oddly, I thought I heard the Lord say in my spirit, *The man next to you has a daughter who is in trouble. Talk to him.*

I tried to remember if I'd eaten anything recently that hadn't been properly refrigerated. *I am making things up,* I told myself. *No way. God doesn't speak to me in this way. I'm exhausted, and I'm going to sleep right now.*

Every time I closed my eyes, I kept getting the same prompt. *The man next to you has a daughter who is in trouble. Talk to him.* The man was sophisticated and elegantly dressed. He had his glasses on, reading *The Wall Street Journal.*

I said to myself, *There is no way I'm going to interrupt this guy while he is reading his paper and say, "Excuse me, sir, is your daughter in trouble?"* I kept trying to fall asleep. It was impossible.

Okay, I reasoned silently, *if this is really God nudging me, I am going to take a chance on totally humiliating myself and ask this perfect stranger about his daughter.*

I turned to the man and said, "Excuse me, sir, is your daughter in trouble?" For an instant his face had a shocked look as if somebody had just doused him with ice water. Then he put his head back, closed his eyes, and started to sob. He let the paper fall into his lap and took off his reading glasses. His shoulders shook and the tears ran down his face.

As soon as he could speak, he turned to me and said, "How could you possibly know that? I have a daughter who is away at college, and she is in terrible trouble. She was a virgin, and she was raped by one of her employers. Now she's pregnant." *No wonder God wouldn't let me take a nap.*

"The best thing I know to do, sir," I said, "is to pray. I don't know what I can say to lighten your burden. But I know that when I don't have the words, God does."

He responded, "Let's pray."

We prayed for his daughter and his family. We prayed for the employer. We prayed for the baby. When we got off the plane, he called his wife immediately and I overheard him say, "We need to commit our lives to God! We need to start praying for our daughter, and we need to go back to church!"

Six months later I was speaking in southern California and, to my delight, this same man came to see me. He came up to me and said, "You have no idea how your prayers changed my daughter's life. She kept the baby—she's going to give it up for adoption—and she's going to church. My wife and I have recommitted our lives to God, and we're back at church too."

My airplane conversation was a divine appointment, but I almost slept through it.

Thank You, Lord, for being persistent, for making me bold enough to risk ridicule to share Your message. All I wanted was a nap, but You had a job for me that brought Your healing hand to an entire family. Help me, like Paul, to ask for boldness, and never think I'm too busy, too tired, or too timid to do Your will. And thank You for showing me the amazing results that take place when I choose to do things Your way.

$\mathcal{T}$HE NEW FATHER FOG

MICHAEL T. POWERS

A father delights in his son.

PROVERBS 3:12

Kristi has been extremely creative in how she tells me I am going to be a father. When she knew she was pregnant with our first son, Caleb, she took me to a nice restaurant for dinner. At the end of our delicious meal, the waitress handed me the bill and a sealed envelope. She told me it was from someone in the restaurant. I looked around, searching for a familiar face, but found none. I opened it and read the typed message.

In the meantime, all the employees, including the chefs from the kitchen, started moving closer to our table.

The message read, "Michael, this is to inform you that you will be changing the kitty litter for the next nine months. In other words, congratulations, you are going to be a father!"

I looked across the table at my beloved wife with disbelief

on my face.

The thought, *How did this happen?!* flashed through my head. I remembered the talk my father had with me long ago, so I knew how it *physically* had happened, but I wanted to know HOW this had happened—why now, finally after waiting so long!

I started bawling like a baby. I had wanted to have children all seven years of our marriage, but Kristi had wanted to wait. This was not something we had planned, and I wasn't emotionally ready for it. There I sat, tears streaming down my face, surrounded by my now crying wife, a bunch of sobbing waitresses, and a couple of chefs who went back into the kitchen in a suspicious hurry.

The next eight months were filled with anticipation and moments of wonder. I remember hearing the sound of my baby's heartbeat. Nothing prepares a man for the moment he hears his child's heartbeat for the first time. It was nothing like I expected. The chugging that came through the speakers sounded just like a train to me. I know that might not sound too exciting or romantic to some people, but to me it was incredible. I remember watching my wife's tummy grow, longing for the day when I would be able to feel Caleb moving inside of her. We would sit for long periods of time, my hands pressed gently against her abdomen, waiting for Caleb to move, but he wouldn't. I would pray that God would give him the hiccups just so I could feel my son through the thin layer that protected him from the outside world.

And then miraculously he moved and I felt him for the first time! I waited breathlessly for him to move again, not believing that it had actually happened. I can't even imagine what it must have felt like for Kristi to sense her offspring moving within her.

As I waited for the day of his birth, I would have dreams of seeing him for the first time; intensely vivid dreams of a baby's face that would stay with me long after sleep ended.

Looking back now, I am amazed at how long, and how short, nine months can be. We never did get to rush off to the hospital like so many people do on TV because Caleb decided he liked it too much inside the womb. After three weeks had past Kristi's due date, the doctors decided to induce labor. So there we sat in the hospital waiting for something to happen.

Labor finally set in—twenty hours of it. And in the end, Caleb's head was too big for the birth canal, and the doctor told us he would have to do a C-section. At this point I was a little worried, but I trusted that God and the doctors knew what they were doing.

And then it finally happened! I was sitting at the head of the operating table, holding Kristi's hand, when the doctor said,

"We have a healthy baby boy." All throughout surgery, I was afraid to stand up so that I could see what was going on. I figured the doctors and nurses would yell at me and say, "Boy, what do you think you are doing?! You sit back down now!" However, when I heard the doctor say that he could see the baby, I didn't care if they threw a scalpel at me; I was going to look at my child.

There he was! I could almost hear the angels singing as my precious baby boy was brought into the world. He was perfect in every way, and the tears began to fall.

"Oh, Kristi! He's beautiful!" was all I could stammer.

I was in the "new father fog."

In reality, Caleb looked terrible. His skin color changed about four times in the first five minutes, and he probably could have made the cover of the *National Enquirer:* "Reptile Boy Born in Wisconsin! Man Fathers Chameleon in Real-Life X-Files Episode!" His hands and feet were extremely wrinkled, like he had been in the pool too long, and all kinds of bodily secretions were oozing from his pores.

Everything else seemed fine, though…. Except for THE TWO HEADS!

Yes, my boy had two heads, and that was the first thing Kristi noticed when the nurse handed Caleb to her for the first time. She told me later that she was thoroughly convinced that she had married a psycho. "My husband called this thing beautiful?"

Because Caleb had gone through twenty hours of labor, but had been too big to fit through the birth canal, it was obvious where his head had been stuck all that time. It had swollen up like a balloon in two different places, and it really did look like he had two heads. Being the proud father that I was, however, I figured that was God's way of helping Caleb to store all the brain matter he'd inherited from me! The swelling did go down in a few days, but Caleb wasn't looking his best for the first few weeks.

It is amazing, though, how being a new father blinded me to certain realities. I kept telling everyone how beautiful he was. It wasn't until a year or so later, after looking at the video, that I realized Caleb had looked like a swollen two-headed lizard that had been in the water for too long. To me though, he was the most beautiful creation that had ever appeared on the earth.

Fatherhood. You gotta love it!

A FATHER'S PRIDE AND JOY

DAVID FLANAGAN

Everything is appropriate in its own time…

[for] God has planted eternity in the hearts of men.

ECCLESIASTES 3:11 TLB

My son's coach recently said, "Your son's quite a ballplayer! You must have spent time playing ball with him because it shows."

I thought about the coach's comments and how Evan's baseball career had started when he was a toddler tossing rocks into the surf for hours on end. Sometimes I would place an old can in the sand and Evan would try to hit the target, which he was amazingly talented at doing.

I remembered how Evan and his brother, David, would turn themselves into tiny corkscrews trying to hit the Wiffle ball off the tee. When Evan was eligible for Little League we signed him up, and before long we realized that he had great skills and a natural ability that he certainly hadn't inherited from me!

Closing my eyes I can see wobbly little legs running around the makeshift diamond in our yard. Little feet traveling a mile a minute, missing the first base rock, lightly tapping the frisbee at second, and scuffing the mound of dirt at third. I would try to hold back my laughter and slow my stride to avoid tagging Evan as he broke for home plate to score the winning run.

Visions of an ecstatic little boy jumping up and down on home plate flashed through my mind, his tiny arms raised in victory, the Sox cap much too big for his head, a mile-wide smile on his face. *God, help us, why do they have to grow up so quickly? Before we know it David and Evan will be off on their own following their dreams wherever they take them.*

The poignant words to the song, "Cat's in the Cradle," by Harry Chapin, move me whenever I hear it. "Cradle" is Chapin's dispirited tale about a guy too engrossed in his own world to make time for his son. But years later, when the old man yearns for a little attention from his adult son, the son just can't seem to fit his dad into his own busy life.

These lyrics stop me in my tracks whenever I hear them, and they encourage me to spend as much time as I possibly can with my children, now, while they are young.

My own father and I have never been very close, and so it's

hard sometimes for me to know how a dad should act and what one should expect from a father-and-son relationship. I may have spent more time with my sons than most fathers do, not necessarily by design but more out of necessity, since my wife works evenings. Regrettably, time waits for no one, and the boys are growing much too quickly, meeting new friends, gaining new interests, and developing a bit of the "wanderlust."

I remember how I would read to the boys and then tuck them in with a kiss goodnight, tugging the covers to make sure that they were snug and warm. As Father's Day approaches I will again remind myself to try to spend as much time as possible with my children because we have no guarantees for tomorrow. I want my sons to know that even though their dad wasn't a perfect father, he always tried his best to become one.

POSTCARDS FROM MY SON

CHARLIE "TREMENDOUS" JONES

How can a young man stay pure?

By reading your Word and following its rules.

PSALM 119:9 TLB

When my son was fourteen, I said, "Jerry, do you want to have a car when you're sixteen?" "Yes." "Do you want me to help you buy that car?" "Yes sir, Dad." "All right, son, we're going to do it, but the free ride's over. No more allowance. Instead, I'm going to give you a way to make a lot of money.

"Here is the deal. I am going to pick out books for you to read. There will be motivational books, history books, inspirational books; every time I give you a book, you give me a book report. Every time I get a book report, I'll put money in your car fund. Another book report—more money in the car fund. In two years if you read in style, you'll drive in style. But if you read like a bum, you're going to drive like a bum."

Overnight my son developed a fantastic hunger for reading! The first book I had him read was Dale Carnegie's *How to Win Friends and Influence People.* The first day he came down and said, "Dad, there's a whole chapter in here on smiling and shaking hands!" And then he shook my hand and smiled at me.

Next I had him read a book about Joshua in the Old Testament and discouragement. As we were going to Sunday school the next week, I asked, "Jerry, how are you getting along with Joshua?" He said, "Dad!" And he playfully hit my leg. Imagine that, he hit my leg! Then he said, "Everybody ought to read that book!" That was a sign he was beginning to think about somebody other than himself.

Well, Jerry read twenty-two books. Did he buy a car? No. He kept the money and used my car and my gas! But it was worth it.

After he went off to college, he began to write me a "Dear Dad" postcard every day for four years. And I could tell that he was thinking thoughts I never dreamed a young person could think. Here's what a few of the postcards said:

"Dear Dad, It's tremendous to be able to know that when you are in a slump, just as a baseball player will break out in time, so will you break out of yours. Yes, time really cures things. Like you said, you don't lose any problems, you just get bigger and better ones, tremendous ones. Tremendously, too. Jerry"

"Dear Dad, Just started reading *A Hundred Great Lives.* Thanks for what you said in the front. The part that every great man never sought to be great. He just followed the vision he had and did what had to be done. Love, Jerry."

"Dad, I just got done typing up little quotes out of the Bible, so everywhere I look, I see them. When people ask me what they are, I tell them they are pinups. Tremendously."

"Dad, I am more convinced than ever that you can do anything you want to. You can beat anyone at anything just by working hard. Handicaps don't mean anything. Because often people who don't have them have a bad attitude and don't want to work."

"Dad, nothing new. Just the same old exciting thought that we can know God personally and forever in this amazing life."

"Dad, when you're behind two papers in the fourth quarter and you're exhausted from the game, you have to make up a set of downs in order to stay in the game. When you get up to the line and you see two, 250-pound tests staring you in the face, it sure is exciting to wait and find out what play the Lord will call next."

A proper diet is good for your body, and good books are good for your mind. So, teach your children to read, read, read!

Their life (and yours!) will be determined by the people they associate with and the books they read. They will come to love many people they will meet in books. Encourage your kids to read biographies, autobiographies, and books on history. Books will provide many of the friends, mentors, role models, and heroes they will need in life. Biographies will help them see that there is nothing that can happen to them that wasn't experienced by many others—people who used their failures and tragedies and disappointments as stepping-stones for more tremendous lives. Many of my best friends are people I've never met: Oswald Chambers, George Mueller, Charles Spurgeon, A.W. Tozer, Abraham Lincoln, Jean Gietzen, and hundreds of others.

But with the Bible, teach your kids to not just read it—but to *study* it! Digest it. Memorize it. God's greatest gift for their time on earth is His Word.

Happy Reading!

A VERY LUCKY MAN

ROY C. GIBBS

(As told to Nancy B. Gibbs)

Marry and have children, and then find mates for them and have

many grandchildren. Multiply! Don't dwindle away!

JEREMIAH 29:6 TLB

Twenty-seven years earlier, I stood before a judge and adopted my twin sons, Chad and Brad. Their mom and I met, fell in love instantly, and we were married in only a few months. Then, two months into our marriage, their biological father gave me the greatest gift I could have ever received. I legally became the father to two precious little boys, after a six-month waiting period.

"You're a very lucky man," the judge announced, as we all stood together as a family before the bench. At that moment, we became a real family. I never knew a family could be so close. I realized that I didn't just marry the love of my life; I was joined by the heart with her sons, as well. Our daughter,

"TO US, FAMILY MEANS PUTTING OUR ARMS AROUND ONE ANOTHER AND BEING THERE."

Barbara Bush

Becky, was born a couple of years later and what a joy she brought to our entire family. The judge was right. I am a very fortunate man.

The kids and I laughed as we played together in the front yard. I coached the boys' football team. Since I am a minister, I had the privilege of baptizing all three of my children after they made decisions to follow Christ. At that moment I became not only their father, but also their brother in Christ. What a wonderful opportunity God had given to me. At times, I forget that I adopted the boys. We have so much in common that I can't imagine a time that we weren't a big happy family.

Before I knew it, the children became teenagers. As they grew older, thankfully, our family grew closer. I tried to give them a firm foundation on which to stand. When the time came for the boys to leave for college, I reluctantly gave them their wings to fly. But I still rejoiced every time they came home for a visit and knew that time and distance would never keep us apart.

After they graduated from college, I again found myself standing before a crowd of people with my son, Chad. As his minister, I conducted his wedding ceremony. Brad stood by his side as his best man, while Becky stood nearby as a bridesmaid. Again, I remembered the words the judge had shared with me a quarter of a century earlier: "You are a very lucky man."

When Chad's beautiful bride, Lucy, joined us, I could barely contain my emotions. I had adopted my son, baptized him, and was also given the opportunity to conduct his wedding ceremony. In addition, we were welcoming a new member to our family—I now had a beautiful daughter-in-law.

Then, approximately a year and a half later, I faced a major illness for the first time in my life. My son Brad was engaged at the time. I had planned to conduct his wedding, as well. But a couple of months before Brad's wedding date, I had open-heart surgery.

Fortunately, with God's blessings, I was well enough to conduct Brad's ceremony. I joined Brad and his beautiful bride, Amy, together as husband and wife. Chad stood beside Brad as his best man. Again, Becky stood nearby as a bridesmaid. I realized again—especially in light of my recent health crisis—how blessed I was as I stood before all my children.

Being a family is much more than simply sharing a name. To be a family means to stand together, support each other, and be there for each other through all the good times and bad times in life, such as baptisms, weddings, anniversaries, and even funerals.

During my lifetime, God has given me many special gifts: He gave me two sons and a beautiful daughter to love forever.

Today, as I reflect upon my sons becoming grooms, I anticipate the time when my daughter, Becky, will become a bride. She will stand before me as I officiate her wedding and we welcome a new son to our family, as well.

The judge was right the day that he signed the adoption papers many years earlier, making me the father of two fantastic sons. I am a very lucky man to have been afforded so many wonderful opportunities as a father and a minister.

God has been good to me, helped me along the way, and showed me the importance of living a life pleasing to Him. Living God's way has not always been easy, but because of the love of my wife and my children I have been challenged to be the man that God wants me to be. I thank God every day for the blessings of my family and home. Yes, Judge...I am a very lucky man.

*T*HE STRANGE ROAD TO SUCCESS

JOE GIBBS

Commit to the Lord whatever you do, and your plans will succeed.

P R O V E R B S   1 6 : 3   N I V

All my life, I wanted to be the head football coach of an NFL team more than anything else.

At times, I even wanted it more than God or my family. I bought right into the world's game plan. In my eyes, being a head coach would give me all the things I wanted, things like money and prestige. My goal became an obsession.

God gave me my first wake-up call in 1972 when I met a small, unassuming Sunday-school teacher named George Tharel while I was coaching at the University of Arkansas. He was a man at peace with himself and God. Being driven was one of my strengths, but I envied people like George who could relax and enjoy life. By looking at George's life, I started to see that there was another game plan besides the world's. God's plan was not based on money, position, or winning football games. God was only concerned with my having a right relationship with Him. And even though I had become a Christian when I was nine years old, I had never made God a priority. George helped me to see this.

One night at church I went forward and confessed that though I knew God, I had not been living for Him. After rededicating my life to God that night, it became evident that things were different. Some of the changes were immediate; others have been a process.

In 1978, my first year as the offensive coordinator for the Tampa Bay Buccaneers, I just knew I was one step away from being a head coach. That was until we finished the season 4 and 12—the first unsuccessful program I'd ever been a part of. After that season, I was offered a job with the San Diego Chargers. The only problem was that the job was not as the offensive coordinator. I would have to be a backfield coach— go backwards in my career—and work under another assistant coach. My pride got in the way and though I took the job, I had no peace about it.

So I decided to go see George back in Arkansas. I got on a plane, but a snowstorm prevented me from making it to see him. I started asking God, *Why? Why is this happening to me?*

Back at the airport, I came across a Bible. I picked it up and turned to the first chapter of James. Out of nowhere, a guy about my age tapped me on the shoulder and said, "I claimed the verses in that chapter about six months ago." Without my having said a word, this guy rattled off a story that paralleled mine almost exactly. He had the job that he'd always wanted, lost it, and tried everything he could do to get it back. Then God, in His timing, gave it back to him.

This was no coincidence! God had brought this guy into my life to show me what I needed to do. So I turned my situation over to God. And within two weeks the offensive coordinator left, opening up the position for me. Two years later, I became the head coach of the Washington Redskins.

One major process God took me through was being able to place my complete trust in Him. When I quit listening to the world's myths about success and happiness and placed my dream of a head-coaching job in God's hands, He completely blessed my life! And even though I've always felt that my family was important, it wasn't until God helped me get my priorities straight in other areas that I realized my wife and family needed to come before my career.

Like anyone else, I wanted to be happy and successful, and that was the path I had been on my whole life. I took the long road but discovered that what I was looking for was not something to be pursued. Success and happiness were by-products of a life given over to God. It seems I had to learn that lesson more than once, and in many ways I'm still learning it.

$\mathcal{A}$ PROMISE KEPT

KRISTI POWERS

If a man vow a vow unto the Lord...he shall not break his word,

he shall do according to all that proceedeth out of his mouth.

NUMBERS 30:2

My father was not a sentimental man. I don't remember him ever "ooohhing" or "ahhing" over something I made as a child. Don't get me wrong—I knew that my dad loved me, but getting all mushy-eyed was not his thing. I learned that he showed me love in other ways.

There was one particular time in my life when this became truly real to me. I had always believed that my parents had a good marriage, but just before I, the youngest of four children, turned sixteen, my belief was sorely tested. My father, who used to share in the chores around the house, gradually started becoming despondent. From the time he came home from his job at the factory until the time he went to bed, he hardly spoke a word to my mom or us kids. The strain on my mom and dad's relationship was very evident. However, I was not prepared for the day that Mom sat my siblings and me down and told us that Dad had decided to leave our home. All I could think was that I was going to be a product of a divorced family. It was something I had never thought possible, and it grieved me greatly. I kept telling myself that it wasn't really going to happen, but I went totally numb when I realized that my dad was actually leaving.

The night before he left, I stayed in my room for a long time. I prayed and I cried—and I wrote a long letter to my dad. I told him how much I loved him and how much I would miss him. I told him that I was praying for him and wanted him to know that, no matter what, Jesus and I loved him. I told him that I would always and forever be his Krissie...his "Noodles." As I folded my note, I stuck in a picture of me with a saying I had always heard: "Anyone can be a father, but it takes someone special to be a daddy."

Early the next morning, as my dad left our house, I snuck out to the car and slipped my letter into one of his bags.

Two weeks went by with hardly a word from my father. Then one afternoon, I came home from school to find my mom sitting at the dining-room table waiting to talk to me. I could see in her eyes that she had been crying. She told me that Dad had been there and that they had talked for a long time. They'd decided that there were things that they could work on, changes they could make—and that their marriage was worth saving. Mom then turned her focus to my eyes—"Kristi, Dad told me that you wrote him a letter. Can I ask what you wrote to him?"

I found it hard to share with my mom what I had written from my heart to my dad. I mumbled a few words and shrugged. And then Mom told me, "Dad said that when he read your letter, it made him cry. It meant a lot to him, and I have hardly ever seen your dad cry. After he read your letter, he called to ask if he could come over to talk. Whatever you said really made a difference to your dad."

A few days later my dad was back, this time to stay. We never talked about the letter, my dad and I. But I knew there was an unspoken promise that he would always be there for me.

My parents went on to be married a total of thirty-six years before my dad's early death at the age of fifty-three, cut short their lives together. In the last sixteen years of my parent's marriage I, and all those who knew my mom and dad, witnessed one of the truly "great" marriages. Their love grew stronger every day, and my heart swelled with pride as I saw them grow closer together.

When Mom and Dad received the news from the doctor that his heart was rapidly deteriorating, they took it hand in hand, side by side, all the way. After Dad's death, we had the most unpleasant task of going through his things. I didn't really want to be involved in that process, and so I opted to run errands while most of Dad's things were divided and boxed up.

When I got back, my brother said, "Kristi, Mom said to give this to you. She said you would know what it meant." As I looked down into his outstretched hand, it was then that I knew the impact that my letter had had that day so long ago. In my brother's hand was the picture I'd given my dad. My unsentimental dad, who never let his emotions get the best of him, my dad, who almost never outwardly showed his love for me, had kept the one thing that meant so much to him— and to me.

I sat down and the tears began to flow, tears that I thought had dried up from the grief of his death, but that had now found new life as I realized what I had meant to him. Mom told me that Dad kept both the picture and that letter his whole life.

In my home I have a box that I call the "Dad box." In it are so many things that remind me of him. I pull that picture out every once in a while and remember. I remember a promise that was made many years ago between a young man and his bride on their wedding day, and I remember the unspoken promise that was made between a father and his daughter....

A promise kept.

SWIMMING ON DADDY'S BACK

GARY STANLEY

Let us hold unswervingly to the hope we profess,

for he who promised is faithful.

HEBREWS 10:23 NIV

"You have to believe that the water will spend more time holding you up than it spends pulling you under," Dad instructed.

It is hard to "believe" when your experience is telling you something else.

"Relax. Don't fight the water; move through it. Keep your mouth shut, your eyes open, and your fingers together."

Dad's words were all but useless. Completely surrounded by water, an odd mix of excitement and fear gripped me. Everything in me wanted to thrash and flail.

"I've got you, Gary. I won't let anything happen," Dad

continued as he supported my small body with his hand.

While I couldn't relax in the water, I could always relax in his hand—and I soon did. The unknown became comfortable in the company of the known, and progress was made in the absence of panic. Dad's presence was stronger than my surroundings. And it wasn't long before I was ready to believe that the water actually *would* spend more time holding me up than it spent pulling me under. I loved the water, and I loved to swim, especially when Dad was around.

"Grab your nose, grab your knees, and take a deep breath!" And with that bit of instruction Dad began to spin me somersault style in about five feet of water. My head shot down and then back up as I made my first complete forward somersault; air and water in the face, a giant hand behind the neck, and the other hand pushing the front of my ankles like the helm of an old pirate ship. The first time we tried it, I only made one revolution before I came out of my tuck and ended the spin cycle, unsure of which way was up. But over time my lung capacity improved right along with Dad's technique. My lifetime record was twenty-two complete revolutions on one breath.

Dad was a great floater. And at 210 pounds he displaced a lot of water! He could propel himself along feet-first with his toes out of the water, and when he did, look out! Crab Toe might get you! Dad had perfected the pinching skill necessary to grab the skin around my middle between his big toe and the next one. When Crab Toe was out and about, the goal was to swim as close as you could without getting caught. We played "crab tag" a thousand times.

"Rest your hands on my shoulders, and don't choke me. Remember, let the water hold you up." Hitching a ride on Daddy's back was like bodysurfing through slow waves. Each of his frog kicks propelled us forward as we dropped lower in the water, and each breaststroke lifted us higher again. I soon learned that if I pushed myself too far out of the water, the added weight forced Dad to swim harder, and my ride was shortened. But if I lay as close as I could, the water supporting my weight, he could swim forever. I tried to make myself so light he'd hardly notice I was there—swimming on Daddy's back. Such great memories!

My wife, Luci, and I had lunch the other day with some new friends, Doug and Amy. They recently adopted two brothers, five and seven years old. Amy told us of the first time she took them to the community pool. "I won't let anything happen to you," Amy assured her two new sons. "Just remember that your arm floaties (the modern version of water wings) will keep you up."

The younger boy took to the water—arm floaties and all— like a baby duck. He knew something about trust because he always had his big brother to look out for him. But the older boy was terrified of the water. Years of foster care had taught him that adults weren't always that trustworthy.

It took several days just to coax him to the edge of the pool where he sat with his feet in the water. Eventually, he allowed Amy to hold him as he clung to her and she stood in the water next to the side of the pool. Then they worked up to the point where she could take him a single step away from the side and then right back again. The day he dogpaddled a whole five feet from Amy's arms back to Doug's embrace, he shouted. "I trusted you! I trusted you, Mommy!"

The boy didn't say, "These arm floaties really work!" though that was true. No, his newfound trust was wrapped tightly around a person—his new mom.

Before any of us can act on the promise that "the arm floaties will hold you up," or that "the water will spend more time holding you up than pulling you under," we have to believe the one who is saying those words. Sometimes it only takes a moment; sometimes it takes a lot longer. Either way, trust is always personal.

Whether you're holding on for dear life or trying to keep a feather touch so light it's hardly noticed, it's the object of your faith, not the size of it that matters.

Trust is like a finely lacquered finish, it is built up one layer at a time.

*T*HE GOAL OF MY LIFE

PAUL HENDERSON

Believe on the Lord Jesus Christ, and you will be saved,

you and your household.

ACTS 16:31 NKJV

They call the winning goal I scored in the last game of the 1972 Canada-Russia hockey series, "The Goal of the Century." I still get a warm feeling when I think about it.

Fear is one of the best motivators, and I was very afraid that I would be part of the team that lost to the Russians. Canada is not a big nation, but hockey is our game. Everyone on the team felt a responsibility to win.

I had confidence that our team was better than the Russians, but it never entered my mind that it would be me who would score that last goal. I wish I could have handled things a little better after that, been more mature. If I'd had a spiritual dimension to my life at the time, I know I would have.

Back then, I had fulfilled most of my boyhood dreams, and I

knew I was a very fortunate and blessed individual. Yet there was a restlessness, a discontentment in the center of my being that I could not ignore. I was angry, bitter, and frustrated, and there were things about my life that I didn't know how to handle. Things were not going well with the Maple Leafs, the team on which I was playing, and I was having some conflicts with the owner. Here I was playing in the NHL, doing something that I had always dreamed of, but I had become more bitter and angry than I had ever been in my life.

I started drinking as a way to soothe the pain. I think that if you are frustrated and angry, you look for a way out. You get with the boys and you try to "make merry," but you wake up the next morning and the pain is still there.

Fortunately, a friend encouraged me to examine the claims of Jesus. He told me that I hadn't taken care of my soul and had never really looked at what was on the inside. That made sense to me, so I started to read the Bible and look into Jesus. Jesus claimed to be the Son of God, and He said He loved me and wanted to give me eternal life. After a two-year search, I became convinced that I should get to know Him.

However, it was a real struggle for me to become a Christian for a number of reasons. First, I had always prided myself in being a self-made man. I was used to being in control of my life. I was also afraid of what my friends would think. And I looked at Christianity as a thing with a list of "dos" and "don'ts" and perceived it to be too narrow for me. *How can I be a "man's man" and still be a Christian?* I wondered. I was worried that I would have to give up too much.

One day I just couldn't fight it any longer. I threw all my fears aside and I said to God, *I am fearful, and I don't want to tell anyone about this.* But then I gave my life to the Lord.

Since that day, I have never been the same. God has had a positive impact in every area of my life. Most importantly, He has taken away the anger and bitterness. My life certainly hasn't been trouble-free. One of the most challenging times in my life was when my wife was in the hospital and we thought she was going to die. I struggled with feelings of anger toward God, but I also realized that life is a gift from Him, and I decided to place everything in my life in His hands.

He has proven Himself to me over the years with His faithfulness, and I know that I have no choice but to surrender my life to Him. Now I have a certain assurance based upon the inner quietness, contentment, and peace I experience on a daily basis, that His promise to love and care for me is true and real. And best of all, I look forward to spending eternity with Him.

Editor's Note: Paul Henderson is now spending eternity with the loving God Who saved him. He passed away in May of 2003, giving testimony to God's grace, and surrounded by his loving family.

DAD'S "COAT OF MANY HORRORS"

TODD AND JEDD HAFER

Honor thy father

EXODUS 20:12

We're often asked, "What's the most embarrassing thing about being a P.K.?" Some people think that it's having Dad use a bedwetting problem in his sermon entitled, "The Great Drought in the Land of Canaan."

Others think it might be when the head deacon stood up in front of the entire congregation and asked, "Todd, was that a holy kiss you were giving my daughter on the front porch last night? Why are you turning red there, boy?"

But truth to tell, what has caused us the most shame is Dad's favorite Sunday preachin' jacket. We're still not sure where he got this piece of apparel. We think it might have been from Winko's Shop for the Tall or Husky Clown.

"OH, TO BE ONLY HALF AS WONDERFUL AS MY CHILD THOUGHT I WAS WHEN HE WAS SMALL, AND ONLY HALF AS STUPID AS MY TEENAGER THINKS I AM NOW."

Rebecca Richards

If you ever visit our church, the jacket is the first thing you'll notice: purple and green double-knit polyester; big ivory moose-head-shaped buttons down the front; a Canadian landscape on the back; and pockets large enough to hold three quarter-pounders—hence, the grease stains.

Over the years, we've hidden the jacket we nicknamed, "The Coat of Many Horrors." But Dad always found it. (One of the woodchucks in the Canadian landscape scene has glow-in-the-dark eyes—thus helping Dad to locate it even in the darkest corners of the attic.)

We tried milder forms of dissuasion, too, such as: "Wow, Dad, that coat is really kinda out of style."

"What? I'll have you know Mrs. Fargutson complimented me on this coat just last Sunday," he would counter. "Good thing *someone* has some fashion sense around here!"

"But Dad," we would wail, "Mrs. Fargutson is eighty years old and wears white go-go boots and a straw hat with plastic fruit on it."

"What's wrong with that? Kind of reminds people of the fruit of the Spirit. Now that you mention it, I may use her hat as a visual aid next Sunday. Hey, thanks guys. That was very helpful."

Finally realizing that logic had sorely failed us, we were forced to resort to sabotage. Extreme measures were in order.

Frankly, it took Todd a few minutes to come to grips with a more drastic solution. He's always been a bit squeamish about doing things that can conceivably alter the course of history. But finally even Todd had to bow to the gravity of the situation. So one Wednesday night while Dad was over at the church for Bible study, we took the "Coat of Many Horrors" and dropped it off at Goodwill.

Imagine our consternation when we found it lying on the porch the next morning with a death-threat letter pinned to the lapel. We don't want to cast aspersions on a fine charitable organization, but that, friends, is *not* "good will"! (Calm down, folks. We made this paragraph up!)

This incident has brought us to a place of acceptance, however. Obviously the "Coat of Many Horrors" has its own special place in the wide spectrum of God's mysterious ways. We're trying to be philosophical about it—at least Dad hasn't tried to squeeze into his 1970s white-and-purple-striped bell-bottoms…yet.

*W*INNING ISN'T ENOUGH

TOM LEHMAN

The grass withers, the flower fades beneath the breath of God.

And so it is with fragile man. The grass withers, the flowers fade,

but the Word of our God shall stand forever.

ISAIAH 40:7-8 TLB

My disappointment was intense as I watched my shot disappear into the bunker on the last hole, and with it, my chances of winning the 1994 Masters. But that was only the beginning of my disappointments. For the next two years I failed to win the U.S. Open, finishing in second place each time. I was struggling with self-doubt, and I dreaded to hear what I knew my critics would say: that I would never win the big one.

These feelings of self-doubt weren't new to me. When I was fifteen years old, our football team won the state championship. I was third-string quarterback, so I just sat on the bench the whole time watching the other guys play. I didn't play a down all year.

When we got back to town, we had a big parade, then went back to the school gym to have a pep rally. Everyone was so excited. They had a big band playing and everybody was hugging and "high-fiving." But I remember just sitting there and feeling completely isolated, because I didn't really help the team win the championship. I felt like I was a failure. I just wasn't good enough. You get that a lot in sports. That sense of, "you're only as good as your last performance."

As I sat there in the gym, the feeling of "I don't matter" was so overwhelming that I could hardly stand it. I had tried my hardest. I had tried to be good for my parents, good for my team, good for my friends, good for God. With each failure, I'd just feel worse and worse. That led to some introspection on my part, which wasn't at all normal for me at the time. I began to think, *What is it that gives life meaning? Why am I here? Why am I so miserable?*

As luck would have it, my coach was a Christian, and he invited me out to a meeting with some Christian athletes. For the first time, I heard people talking about God and the unconditional love He has for us, the unconditional acceptance He has for us. I thought that was exactly what I was looking for. I wanted to feel that I was loved, that I was valued despite my failures. With God, I suddenly realized that I mattered enough to Him that He died for me. That was an incredible thought. It choked me up, and it made me realize that I was important.

Right then I asked God to come into my life. And I've never had a feeling like that since. The feeling of guilt on my shoulders just disappeared. I felt peace and contentment like I had never known.

Shortly after I lost the two U.S. Opens, I won the British Open and the PGA Tour Championship. I was even ranked the best player in the world. But after all the celebrations, I was the same person with the same problems. You think victory will change your life, that life's going to be better because you won a golf tournament. But when things are all over, you are still faced with the ever evolving issues of life, and you even have added complications from all the sudden notoriety.

The Bible says that all men are like grass and their glory like the flowers of the field. The grass withers and the flowers fade. I found this to be true in my life. Victory is great, but it is ultimately empty. Even the thrill of winning the British Open fades.

So what does last? My relationship with God and with others. They are what gives life meaning. Regardless of what anyone says about me or how I feel about myself, my wife and kids think I'm great. They love me. But more importantly, God loves me. And, ultimately, He's the only One who matters.

*G*OD TOOK ME IN

KEN FREEMAN

My father and mother walked out and left me, but God took me in.

PSALM 27:10 THE MESSAGE

None of the stepfathers and strangers who meandered through my life filled the simple need I had for a father. I hungered for someone who would teach me how to throw a ball, play catch with me, take me fishing, show me how to build a campfire, read me a bedtime story, and reassure me with a hug. I needed a father to show affection for my mother so I could know the security of a stable, loving home. I needed someone who would work hard so I could have adequate physical nourishment and provision. Most importantly, I needed a father to demonstrate responsibility so I would know how to act like a man.

I didn't have any of those things from my father. I don't know exactly when he left: One day I just realized he was gone. When I asked Mom where Dad was, she growled, "He's gone, and he ain't comin' back." Oh, how I missed Dad! None of my nine stepfathers could fill the void—not even the stepfather who stayed around the longest.

This stepfather even played a little baseball with me, although I was usually such an emotional bundle of nerves that I struggled to enjoy it. I placed intense pressure on myself to perform. I thought if I did well, others would like me and want to be my friend. I even managed to make a Little League team one summer.

For years I thought all men were idiots and worthless drunks. The only male role models I had ever known were shiftless, dishonest vagabonds whose primary joy in life was winning a poker hand. Though I detested these men, unfortunately, I was on the road to becoming just like them. Taking up smoking and drinking at the age of ten, I learned how to lie, cheat, and steal with the skill of a seasoned, small-time jailbird.

This kind of influence stirred an inward anger that fueled my disrespect for rules and a contempt for anyone in authority. I hated my father because he wasn't around. And I hated the other men who drifted in and out of our lives. After my parents divorced, every man Mom married was someone she met in a tavern. I don't know if any of them ever held steady jobs because they usually walked around with hangovers. I greeted each new stepfather with hope, but it didn't take long before I came to despise the fact that instead of one drunk parent at home, there were two, which doubled the intensity of the fighting and swearing.

I learned to drive at thirteen because of my parents' irresponsible behavior. We were on our way home one night when one of my stepfathers suddenly slumped over the wheel. Reaching from the backseat, I frantically shook him by the shoulder. Startled, he smacked the brakes and jerked the car off to the side of the road. Finally, he got out of the door, stumbled, and fell on the pavement. After wavering to his feet, he climbed into the backseat. I crawled up front and drove us home, my hands shaking as I strained to see over the wheel.

All this happened in the fifties and sixties, that supposedly blissful era that spawned such feel-good television shows as *Leave It to Beaver, Father Knows Best, Dennis the Menace,* and *The Andy Griffith Show.* To this day I love watching the reruns, especially of Andy Griffith. Andy was a great father and Opie always called him, "Pa." Andy represented the father I had wanted so badly.

I often imagined how great it would be to have a dad who came home sober and spent time with his family. But most of the time I just watched television and daydreamed about a true family. This reverie provided a tidbit of imaginary security. Blocking out reality, I would muster enough strength to make it through another day, hoping that someday I would lead a normal life.

But I didn't give myself much hope and neither did anyone else.

Then I met Jeff.

Jeff McGowan was a defensive lineman on the high-school football team. We called him Cowboy because he wasn't afraid of anything or anybody—even though at only six feet tall and less than two hundred pounds, he wasn't all that big. He wasn't conceited over his status as a football star. Everyone liked Jeff, who was president of the Christian club at school. Like me, he came from a broken home, but he didn't seem soured by his past. That impressed me. He had an awesome way of relating to other people. I wanted to be more like Jeff, but I just didn't know how.

Jeff kept inviting me to church and each time, I invented a creative excuse not to go. After several rejections, Jeff told me that an evangelist named Freddie Gage was coming to his church. To persuade me to come, he mentioned that they were serving pizza and that some of the girls I liked would be there. As usual, I made a lame excuse.

To my surprise, however, Jeff showed up at my front door

later that day with a resolute look on his face.

"Dude, you're goin'," he proclaimed.

I thought a moment. He was bigger than I was. I didn't mind getting some free pizza. It was a chance to meet a few babes.

"Okay," I nodded.

As we drove downtown to the church, I plotted my escape. As soon as I had a chance to eat, I would sneak out the back door. When we arrived, I felt a twinge of nervousness. The only time I had been inside a church before was to steal something or to set wastebaskets on fire. I didn't really know anything about God, and I wondered if my former pranks would come back to haunt me. I felt like an invader in the enemy's camp.

In spite of my cigarette-soaked, repulsive-smelling clothing, nobody shunned me. I was pleasantly surprised by everyone's friendliness.

Then, I found out the pizza would be served after the service, not before. And Jeff didn't intend to give me a chance to dart out early. He followed me around like a hawk before suggesting we go inside the sanctuary and find a seat. *All right,* I told myself, *I'll get through this, meet some people, and then never do this thing again.*

I followed Jeff as he walked up to the front, onto the stage, and into the choir section! At first, I thought it was a joke. But everyone in the choir hugged me and treated me like an old friend. Soon the music started, transforming me into a choir member. I sang some familiar hymns, such as "Amazing Grace." When I didn't know a song, I stuck my head behind the book or mouthed the words silently until I picked up the tune.

When the music stopped, I analyzed the situation. Looking down at the bottom of the first page of the hymnal and seeing that the song had been written in 1732, I almost burst into laughter. These oddballs were singing songs nearly 250 years old!

The music wasn't the only thing I found amusing. When it started and the director stood up, dramatically waving his arms, I thought he was having back spasms. These folks were definitely weird. Especially those who hugged me and said, "We love you, brother!" *I don't even know who your mom is,* I thought, *so how did I become your brother?* Then the evangelist came onstage.

At first I didn't take Freddie Gage seriously, despite his dramatic opening line: "All my friends are dead." Gage went on to describe how he grew up on the streets of Houston, abusing drugs and running with a gang. Because he had turned his life over to God, he said, he was the only gang member who had survived to age twenty-five. After God turned his life around, Gage had gone back to the bars, but *now* he stood on pool tables to preach.

"Some of you have been drinking, doing drugs and messing up your life," he said, a remark that startled me. *How did he know what I'd been doing?*

I thought Jeff had somehow slipped out before the service and told the evangelist all about me before he went onstage. And now, there he was, spilling my secrets to the whole church!

Then, the congregation got me laughing again, by shouting "Amen!"

Yet as he spoke, I could see that he really believed what he was saying. His passion and intensity in his belief in God was reflected in his eyes. I thought, *if someone is this serious about God and could believe in Him that strongly, maybe I should listen.* I quit thinking about the petty things that had distracted me and started paying attention to this fiery evangelist.

"God's got a purpose for your life," he pointed out. My heart thumped. *A purpose? For me?* "God loves everybody," he continued. "There's nothing you've done or could do that would keep God from loving you. But you've got to receive Him and believe in Him."

I thought about the times I had tried to commit suicide or daydreamed about killing myself. My mind wandered back over all the drugs, drinking, crime, and shattered dreams that had dominated my life. Maybe there *was* an answer—a way out of this mess. Maybe *God* was the answer. Maybe this evangelist wasn't such a goofball. After all, he had come from the streets of Houston. If he could turn his life around, maybe I could too.

I began to weep as the evangelist neared the end of his message. All the emotional garbage of the past surfaced and melted my heart. I may have hardened myself on the outside, but inside I knew the truth: I was hurting. I wanted relief from the pain. Still, there was a fierce tug-of-war going on inside me. This evangelist's message had touched me, but I wasn't too sure of what was happening. When he asked everyone to bow their heads, I only half-bowed mine. I was determined to keep an eye on things.

"If you'd like to have what I have, stand up," he said.

Without thinking or realizing what I was doing, I stood. For the first time in my life, I didn't care what anyone else thought. When Gage invited those who had stood up to walk to the altar where he was standing, I obeyed.

"Son, do you know you're a sinner?" he asked. The first thing I wanted to say was, "I'm not your son." Instead, I shook my head and said, "Sir, I don't know what I am. All I know is my mom wants me dead. She thinks I came from hell, and I haven't seen my dad in more than a dozen years. I don't have a real family, and I've got a stepdad who is a drunk. I've tried suicide. That's all I know. If this Jesus can make my life better, then I want to know Him."

He guaranteed me Christ could do that.

"Will this Jesus ever leave me?" I asked.

"You might turn your back on Him, but He will never turn His back on you."

That convinced me. At his urging, we knelt to pray. I would have done anything he asked, from turning cartwheels to performing jumping jacks. I trusted this guy and I wanted what he had.

At that moment God touched and transformed my life.

When I knelt to pray with that evangelist, God saw my hungering faith and I accepted His free gift of salvation by faith in His Son, Jesus Christ.

Looking back, I am thankful for the friendship of a school friend…who reached out to me. But most of all to God, who reached all the way down to a messed-up sixteen-year-old in the choir loft and gave me a brand-new life—one that still amazes, thrills, and satisfies me.

*W*INNING WAYS

MICHAEL CHANG

Every good gift and every perfect gift is from above,

and comes down from the Father of lights.

JAMES 1:17 NKJV

They said I was too small, that I didn't have the strength, that I wouldn't cut it. I'll admit it's been tough—really tough. Sometimes I still feel I just don't have the height or strength to go out and compete against the bigger guys.

But I found it takes a lot more than physical size or strength to make it in life—both on and off the court. That's where I found having a relationship with God makes all the difference.

At fifteen years of age, I was doing a lot of searching. I think at that age, teens naturally wonder about the meaning of life and are really trying to find themselves. I definitely had a lot of questions.

I became a Christian in 1988. My grandparents had given

me a Bible that they asked me to read every day. On one particular evening when I didn't have anything else to do, I decided to take a good look at it and see what it had to say. I found the Bible to be true and pure, expressing incredible love and peace through the life of Jesus Christ. Through my reading, I eventually accepted Jesus as my Lord and Savior.

When I won the 1989 French Open—my first Grand Slam title—I was only seventeen. This came much earlier than my family and I ever dreamed. I never expected it, and I don't think anyone else in the tennis world expected it either. But the Lord has His way of working things out.

It might have been easy to let my head swell, getting caught up in the money, fame, and glamour of winning. I am thankful that I was able to stay focused on Jesus and not fall into that trap. I believe that I have been put in this position in order to touch people's lives in a positive way. Nothing is as important to me as this.

I also consider it fortunate that I became a Christian the first year that I was on the tour. Before all the fame and money, the Lord had been teaching me His ways. It is wonderful to be able to look back at my life before I was a Christian and see how even then the Lord was being watchful over my life.

I know God is the One who gave me the ability to play tennis. I would not be where I am without His having given me the strength to play the way I do. What's important is giving it my best. I may win or I may lose, but when I keep my focus on Him, I always have the joy He alone can give.

I have confidence knowing that everything is in His hands. I have seen so many things happen in my life that I know are not mere coincidences. I know that the Lord loves me and that He will always be with me looking out for me—no matter what happens.

$\mathcal{R}$EDEFINING SUCCESS

ED BECKER

Therefore if any man be in Christ, he is a new creature:

old things are passed away; behold all things are become new.

2 CORINTHIANS 5:17

In 1977, I thought I was successful. I owned 50 percent of a successful business, had a Ph.D., and was married with three children. I believed that I had accomplished this all through my own capability and wisdom. I thought I could accomplish anything if I just tried hard enough. My knowledge, strength of will, college degrees, and business success were important to me, and I put them ahead of everything else.

My twenty-year-old son, Alan, had different priorities. He tried to tell me what Jesus Christ meant to him, but I was convinced I didn't need Him. I told Alan that I could do everything myself. I was so firm about rejecting the Christian faith that Alan told his pastor, "My dad will never become a

Christian!"

As a chemical engineer, I had tried to prove or disprove the existence of God based upon the same criteria as one tests chemical reactions in a lab. The tests came up empty, so I ignored God.

Sometime later, Alan became seriously ill and was admitted to the hospital. After his heart stopped beating, I stood outside the emergency room struggling with pain, anguish, and helplessness. It was then that I realized I could not do everything myself. There was nothing I could do as my son hovered on the brink of death. I didn't even know how to pray.

Alan survived the cardiac arrest, but he was in the hospital for a long time suffering from a serious infection. But he told me, "God is in charge." I was astonished and deeply moved by his faith and trust in God.

I began reading Alan's Bible to him every day at his bedside. For the first time, I began to learn what the Bible was really about. And I began to learn about Jesus. Alan's strong belief in Christianity, combined with what I read in the Bible, made me realize that Jesus was real. Although I tried in years past to believe that Jesus was nothing more than a great teacher or prophet, a month after Alan's accident, I asked Christ to take charge of my life, to be my Lord and Savior. I knew God wanted me to have a more purposeful life and that this was the first step toward a life with true meaning. Alan was thrilled when I told him about my decision! He had prayed for a long time that his father would know eternal life.

Three weeks after my decision, Alan went into a coma. For three days I hardly left his bedside, until finally he slipped away from this life on earth to be with his Lord and Savior. I had looked forward to sharing my new Christian life with my son, but I knew that he would now spend eternity in Heaven and that I would see him again someday. Though grief-stricken, God gave my wife and me a peace and hope that surpassed all human understanding.

The Bible says in 2 Corinthians 5:17 that if anyone is in Christ, he is a "new creation." The old self has gone and the new has come. This certainly was true in my life. God now has first priority, followed by my wife and family, and then my business. My principles for decision-making have also changed completely. I ask God for help in making daily business decisions, and no longer rely solely on my own knowledge. I have found that God's infinite wisdom is vastly superior to my own. Best of all, there is an unspeakable joy in my life no matter what may come, because I know that I have eternal life to look forward to.

*W*ITHOUT FEAR

ROGER NEILSON

God has not given us the spirit of fear, but of love, power, and a sound mind.

2 TIMOTHY 1:7

I still remember the look on the team doctor's face when he announced that I had multiple myeloma, a deadly cancer that had claimed the life of my sister only four years prior. Up to that point I had been pretty fortunate in that I'd always been reasonably healthy. But now it looked like I would have to give up coaching. Worse, I probably only had two or three years to live.

Things looked pretty bad, but they didn't stay that way for long. My doctor told me not to worry about dying just yet. He prescribed a regimen of chemotherapy and arranged for a stem cell transplant.

"That will keep you around for the next four or five years, for sure," he said. "By then, they'll have come up with some new things to help you."

I was really encouraged by this news, especially once I found out I could keep coaching for the next two or three months. It's been a year now since I was diagnosed with cancer. I'm in remission and off all medication. The most important thing that got me through it all was my faith in God. Without that, it would have been extremely difficult. There were so many times when I was lying in the hospital wondering if I'd ever get out. I would cry out to God and ask for His help. And somehow, something always happened that made things better. I knew all along that the Lord was with me and that whatever happened, I could trust Him to get me through it.

That's been true in my life a number of times, not only with the cancer. I've been fired from eight or nine hockey teams. When you're fired in professional sports, it's a national thing—everybody knows about it. It's not easy, but knowing that God had a plan for my life gave me the ability to handle life's disappointments. The difficult situations didn't always go away, but He gave me the grace and the wisdom to deal with them.

Finding out that you have cancer is tough. However, as a Christian, I know that no matter what I go through, God is always with me. I know that if I trust in God then I don't have to worry about the future—it's in His hands. I've known the

Lord since I was a young boy, and I've always felt that death is not something to be afraid of. Knowing Jesus means that when I leave this life, I'm going to Heaven. I've got a place to go when it's all over. And that's the only way to go.

Editor's Note: Roger Neilson is now in Heaven. He died on May 18, 2003, surrounded by loving friends and family.

*P*INTO BEANS AND FRIED BOLOGNA—NOW THAT'S A FEAST OF FAITH!

STAN TOLER

Blessings in the city, blessings in the field;...

Blessings when you come in, blessings when you go out.

DEUTERONOMY 28:3-6 TLB

Growing up in the hills of West Virginia made a tremendous impact on my life. My dad was a coal miner, and we lived in a coal mining community—Baileysville, unincorporated. Of course, most towns in West Virginia are still unincorporated. And the population of Baileysville was down to sixty as of 1994, so it will probably never be incorporated! In fact, it's so small that Main Street is a cul-de-sac. But it is still my hometown.

Californians love to brag about being able to go to the mountains to snow ski and to the ocean to sunbathe in the same day. Well, in Baileysville, we had our own definition of the good life. If you lived on the side of the mountain, you could cross the river any day, anytime, on an old-fashioned swinging bridge!

My Saturdays were spent at the Wyoming Company Store. While Mom and Dad made purchases with coal mining dollars, I was in charge of watching my brothers, Terry and Mark. That wasn't difficult if you knew what to do. We eagerly peered at the black and white television sets in the furniture department. Programs such as *Fury, SkyKing,* and *My Friend Flicka* seemed so real to us!

Our small white frame house was located on the side of Baileysville Mountain. We had a well nearby that provided ample water and a pot-bellied coal stove to keep us warm (as long as you remembered to put the coal in it!).

I have heard that someone can be described as a "redneck" if his bathroom requires a flashlight and shoes. Well, our little house had three rooms and a path to the little house out back. But it was our home, and I loved it—no matter how red it made my neck!

So one of the saddest days of my childhood was a Saturday morning when we returned home from a visit to the company store to see our tiny home engulfed in flames. We lost everything. I cried for days.

By the time I was eleven years old, we had moved to Columbus, Ohio, in search of a better life. My dad, only thirty-one years old, had already broken his back three times in the coal mines and was suffering from the dreaded miners' disease, "black lung." But we were happy and almost always had pinto beans, cornbread, and fried bologna for supper. (That's right, only later did we call it *dinner!*)

Christmas Day, 1961, in Columbus will always be one of the most wonderful, life-changing days in my memory bank. It had been a long, hard winter with lots of snow and cold weather. Times were tough. Dad had been laid off from construction work, our food supply had dwindled to nothing, and we had closed off most of the house from the heat in order to cut down our high utility bills.

My epiphany began Christmas Eve when Mom noted that we had no food for Christmas Day and had no hope of getting any. That was difficult for me to understand. We were used to Mom calling out, "Pinto beans, cornbread, and fried bologna. Come and get it!" But now we didn't even have that. There was no food at all in the house.

Mom suggested that it was time for us to accept a handout from the government commodity department, so—reluctantly—Dad loaded Terry, Mark, and me into our old Plymouth, and we headed downtown. When we got there, we stood in line with hundreds of others for what seemed like hours, waiting for government handouts of cheese, dried milk, flour, and dried eggs. Ugh! The wind was cold, and the snow was blowing as we stood there shivering. Finally, Dad could stand it no longer.

"We're going home, boys. God will provide!" he said. We cried, yet we completely trusted Dad's faith in God.

That night, we popped popcorn and opened gifts that we had ordered with Top Value trading stamps which Mom had wisely saved for that purpose. Some of you may be too young to remember Top Value stamps, but back then, grocery stores gave out trading stamps for purchases made. You could save the stamps and fill up Top Value books for redemption of gift items from their catalog. Mom saved stamps all year long, counted the bounty by November 1, and let us Toler boys pick out our Christmas presents.

Terry got a transistor radio. (He hadn't realized that we had no money to purchase a battery!) I had ordered a miniature Brownie Kodak camera. (That wasn't smart, since we couldn't afford film either!) And baby brother, Mark, got a small teddy bear. While none of the gifts were a surprise to us, Mom had carefully and lovingly wrapped each one to be opened Christmas Eve. We were grateful to have anything!

Everyone slept well under Grandma Brewster's handmade quilts that night. While we were fearful of the prospect of the next day without food, we were just happy to be together as a family. (Little did we know that Dad would be in Heaven by the following Christmas.)

On Christmas morning, December 25, 1961, we were all asleep in Mom and Dad's bedroom, when suddenly, we were startled by a loud knock and a hearty, "Merry Christmas!" greeting from people who attended the Fifth Avenue Church. There stood Clair Parsons, Dalmus Bullock, and others with gifts, clothes, and a thirty-day supply of food. (Yes, dried pinto beans, cornmeal, and a huge roll of bologna were included!) Since that day, I have always believed that God will provide, and that God is *never late* when we need a miracle!

*F*REED FROM RELIGION

BILLY DIAMOND

With God all things are possible.

MARK 10:27

My childhood was a happy one. I recall having a very free and secure life, being loved and taken care of by my family. I had a real sense of security when I traveled with my parents on hunting trips and helped them with their trap lines. But that all changed when I was seven years old. My father put me on an airplane and sent me to a residential school far away from home. I was devastated. In that one day, all those years of being loved, those years of peace and security were ripped apart. I felt that no one loved me anymore, that no one cared about me. I felt as though my parents had abandoned me.

As a result, I grew up with a lot of anger inside. At the same time, I was constantly searching for love. I wanted to know that someone cared about me. The pain that built up inside of me during my teenage years carried on into my adult life. I developed a "wall"—an attitude that I was never going to let anyone hurt me again. And I vowed that I would make a success of my life, that I would never be defeated. I took this attitude with me when I became the leader of my people.

I grew up watching my father as the chief of our community. People had great respect for him as a man of wisdom, leadership, and integrity. As a young boy I acted as a translator for his dealings with provincial and federal politics. Later, he began to groom me to take his place as leader of our community and, eventually, the entire Cree tribe in northern Quebec.

I became chief of our Cree community when I was twenty-one. Around this time many preachers and evangelists wanted to come onto the reserve and share the gospel message. I did everything I could to stop the gospel from coming in, because I remember as a child at school being taught that God was a menacing, huge, punishing being. There could be no real, personal relationship with that type of God.

Four years later, I became the first Grand Chief of the Cree Grand Council. I used this position to help my people develop and grow. We modernized our villages, built houses and schools, and encouraged good health and economic development. I was very successful in my position. However, like all successes, if you don't maintain a healthy balance, there can be serious drawbacks. This simple principle began to reveal itself in my personal life.

I became very proud. Alcohol and drugs took their toll. I lost contact with my family, with my young wife and children. I knew I had to do something. Even with all the success there was a huge void in my life. Instead of a sense of accomplishment, there was an emptiness, a lack of peace.

Then one day my wife told me she had accepted Jesus Christ as her personal Savior. I said "Never. Not me!" I thought it was a white man's religion and I wanted nothing to do with it.

But in the latter part of my term as Grand Chief, things got so bad that one day I cried out to God and asked Him to come into my life and forgive me for my sins.

Things changed drastically after that. I no longer had the desire for alcohol, and the other destructive behaviors that had dominated my life. My wife and I were reconciled, our dying son was healed, and our community was changed as the Gospel came alive in the hearts of my people. I learned that God is a loving Father. That He's a forgiving God, He's a healing God, and He's a Friend with whom you can have a relationship.

Now I know that through Christ people can be changed. With Him, all things are possible.

If you feel like your life isn't going anywhere; like you're stuck in a rut, and you're tired of religion, ceremonies, and rituals open your heart and let God touch you and develop a meaningful relationship with Him. Your life will be transformed into one of purpose and significance and you will never be the same again.

No TIME TO LIVE

JOE H. STARGEL

With Gloria Cassity Stargel

Do not be wise in your own eyes; fear the Lord and shun evil. This will bring health to your body and nourishment to your bones.

PROVERBS 3:7-8 NIV

I don't have time for this, I fretted while checking into the hospital that wintry morning. *The City Council meets next week, my Marine Reservist duty weekend is coming up, and my desk at the office is piled high.*

Regardless, I followed the doctor's orders, and the next day found myself strapped down on a gurney in the surgery recovery room, invaded on all sides by needles and tubes, while a twelve-inch vertical incision on my abdomen—held together with wire stitches—dared me to move.

Hours later, after the attendants had wheeled me back to my room, I managed with great physical effort to ask my wife, Gloria, "What did they do?"

"They removed a large tumor," she answered, carefully avoiding the word *cancer*.

As she smoothed my brow with her fingertips, I drifted back into the anesthetized world from where I'd come. I never pushed for details. I would learn soon enough the unspeakable agony—both physical and mental—in the months yet to follow.

The date: February 8, 1973. The enemy? Reticulum cell sarcoma, a rare cancer of the lymph system, described as "somewhere between Hodgkin's Disease and leukemia."

The prognosis? A 5 percent chance of slowing the fast-multiplying cells.

The possibility for a cure? None.

The life expectancy? Between six weeks and six months.

I had joined the Marine Corps at age seventeen. Now at forty-five I was still an active reservist. Basic training had taught me how to defend myself against an enemy. But nothing had prepared me to fight this sneaky, insidious *thing* that had attacked my body. It soon became apparent: Since the medical community had no answers, this would take spiritual warfare for which I felt woefully unprepared.

Years earlier, when I was released from active duty with the Corps, I had plunged into finding work and trying to catch up on the schooling I'd missed.

At the same time, Gloria and I were in love, and we married

soon after she turned eighteen. The two of us had the same goals: a home and family. When our sons Randy and Rick were born, we felt we had finally realized our dreams.

Somewhere in the process, however, my life had gotten out of kilter. A workaholic and a loner, I devoted more and more of my time to getting further ahead: a hundred-mile commute at night for two law degrees, nine years on the City Commission, two years as mayor, monthly weekend drills with the Marine Corps—a two-week camp every summer. Plus my full-time job as corporate counsel with a road construction firm.

My various careers left little time for my wife and children, or even God for that matter. Still, I considered myself a loving husband, a good father, and an acceptable Christian. Didn't I work twelve hours every day just to provide for my family? Didn't I go to church most Sunday mornings? Wasn't that enough?

When cancer struck, reality struck, as well. Almost without me realizing it, my family had changed—Randy now a college junior; Rick, a high-school senior; Gloria, a wife I hardly knew; and me lacking any spiritual strength.

I began fighting cancer the only way I knew how: *Stay busy. Try not to think about it. Maybe it'll just go away.*

Just home from the hospital, frail, and fourteen pounds thinner, I told Gloria, "I want you to drive me to the City Commission meeting today."

"You can't be serious," she responded. "You're in no shape to go out. The temperature is below freezing, and flu germs are everywhere. Please don't go."

"If you won't drive me, I'll call the police chief to come get me."

The thought of a blue-and-white police car pulling into our driveway, with lights flashing on top, evidently convinced her. She reluctantly drove me to City Hall.

But my show of courage was only for the public. At home, full of fear and self-pity, I withdrew into my shell, allowing no one to get close, not even my family.

Three weeks after surgery the oncologist began chemotherapy, which caused indescribable nausea, extreme weakness, deep depression, and numbness in my fingers and toes. At times I could not walk through the house without holding onto a chair or the doorframe.

After I had survived the six-months-to-live estimate, the doctors administered cobalt treatments—maximum dosage radiation to my torso, front, and back—a procedure fraught with peril as they attempted to kill the marauding cancerous cells without killing me. Again, both nausea and depression overwhelmed me.

Following that year of debilitating treatments, my oncologist adopted a "wait-and-see" policy. He offered no hope, however, for long-term remission. Living with a ticking time bomb, I bore the ever-present fear that the cancer would reactivate at any moment

As the months wore on, my "born-to-worry" wife began to wear a sort of peace on her countenance. A sort-of "I-know-a-secret" smile.

Finally, I could stand it no longer. I found her in the kitchen, peeling potatoes for a casserole. "How is it," I asked her, "that with my life in jeopardy, you can look so serene?"

"Because," she said, setting the pan of potatoes on a burner, "I believe God is going to heal you, just like He healed people in Bible days."

"How can you believe that?" I questioned, pulling up a chair to the table. "You heard what the doctor said."

"Because," she said, joining me. "I've been studying in the Bible about God's love for us, about His promises to us. I've been reading other inspirational books, books telling about modern-day miracles."

"So?" She had my undivided attention.

"So," she said, "I'm convinced God still heals today, just like He did in New Testament days. Joe, I feel in my heart, He is going to heal *you*."

"Why didn't you tell me all this?" I asked as I picked up the newspaper that I had just laid down.

"Because you never talk to me," she came back. "What little time you are home, the newspaper or television comes first."

Ouch! A loner like me was never too receptive of heart-to-heart talks.

Following through on her belief, Gloria enlisted prayers for me from every interested person. She must have bombarded Heaven's gates with prayer requests for my life.

Her optimism proved contagious. I sometimes felt more positive myself. And I began asking myself, *just what are my priorities?*

It took time, but finally this Marine recognized his illness as one dynamite of a wake-up call—a Heaven-played reveille, if you will. *Joe, my boy,* the message was clear, *you've had it all backwards. As important and necessary as work is, a truly successful person puts God first, family second, and work last.*

Some months later, it is a typical Sunday afternoon as I join Gloria in the den. "Honey," I interrupted her reading, "are you ready for our walk? We have enough time before the church service."

Yep. This workaholic, with God's crucial help and his wife's faithful support, heard his wakeup call. Heard it loud and clear. *Take time to live!*

After the Stargels lived under the cloud of cancer for ten years, the oncologist said—in a tone of amazement—"Joe, it's official. I think we'll tell the computer that you're well."

*L*IKE A ROCK

JAY COOKINGHAM

He alone is my rock and my salvation; he is my fortress,

I will never be shaken.

P SALM 6 2 : 2

It was a carefully planned speech, made secretly on an old
reel-to-reel tape player. On it he was spewing tales of bitterness,
anger, and disgust. The shame of being abused by his father, the
anger of being ignored by his family, and the lost hope for
things to ever get better, all recorded in graphic detail with
nothing held back. Along with those details came the
description of the measured madness he would carry out on
himself. A madness that by the time the tape was discovered,
would be far too late to stop. He was saying a final goodbye,
but there was nothing "good" in any of it.

He placed the tape on his pillow in his room, grabbed his
backpack, and left the house that had caused him so much

"WE MUST
ACCEPT
FINITE
DISAPPOINT-
MENT, BUT
WE MUST
NEVER LOSE
INFINITE
HOPE."

*Martin Luther
King Jr.*

pain. Inside his backpack was some stuff to get high and a freshly sharpened hunting knife that, ironically, had been given to him by his father. In the woods nearby was a huge boulder in the middle of a small clearing, one of his favorite places to go. It was here he came to think, to cry, and to hide; today it would be the place he came to die.

He figured that his party buddies would find him first, but that thought brought neither comfort nor sadness to him. He was already too high to feel the results of his actions or to fear the outcome.

For years he'd groaned with the despair of feeling dead on the inside, praying that the misery would stop. He pulled the sharp, shiny blade from its sheath and put its coldness to his wrist. Soon, his pain would end and the bitter taste of hopelessness with it. Even now, the thought of being just a distant echo in someone's memory shrouded his heart in a resignation cry, *No one will care!*

As the blade began to press against his skin, suddenly there was a sound that seemed to come from all around him. One single word was spoken that shook him to instant soberness: the word, *Don't.* Only once was the word spoken, yet it so unnerved the young man that he couldn't finish his task. He had gone into the woods by himself, yet he was not alone.

He slid the knife back into its sheath, placed it inside his backpack, and returned home. He took the tape and destroyed it before it and his former intentions could be discovered. He had not come to know God and yet he had heard His voice and was heading in the right direction.

Some thirty-odd years ago, I was that young man. What I found in that hopeless, dark, and lonely place that day was hope; when the Father said *Don't,* I instantly knew that God was proclaiming the value He placed on my life. He pierced my personal darkness with the intense truth of my worth. Oh, I still struggled with it for a few years afterwards and wrestled mightily until He finally pinned my heart. However, the spark of hope was spoken to me on top of a rock in the woods, finally bursting into flames of renewal when I surrendered all that I was.

Through suicide, I was prepared to deliver myself with what I thought was mercy, but God called out real eternal, redeeming mercy with the simple word, *Don't.* The impact of that word was changing me, even the debris surrounding my life, He was determined to clean up. It was a reminder that enough blood had been spilt, His Son's. What had already come from the Lord's veins changed all of eternity. And with that He also changed the direction of my life forever.

God speaks hope in all He does. Hope infuses us with the strength to stand in difficult times; it fills us with grace to allow

His will to change us.

Hope gives us the ability to believe even though no evidence exists, that we can see.

On top of a rock, alone in the woods, desperate for hope, the God of all creation spoke hope into my life, and I haven't been the same since.

$\mathcal{H}$EAVEN'S REWARDS

NANCY B. GIBBS

Many good works I have shown you from My Father.

JOHN 10:32 NKJV

When my father was a child, his family wasn't wealthy. Many times he was forced to seek work to earn enough money to feed his three younger brothers. He never complained, however, because of his great love for his family.

Even so, the older he got, the more difficult his burdens became. His father had abandoned the family, leaving them penniless, so Daddy became the man of the house. At the tender age of seventeen, he quit school and joined the service. His checks were sent home to support his mother and brothers.

After serving his term in the military, he returned home to marry his high-school sweetheart, my mother. The two of them made a home for themselves, and after several years of marriage my brother was born. Daddy had a way of looking into the future. He wanted his children to have the security that he never had. His main goal in life was to be able to support us and to give us anything we would ever need. But he realized that for this to be accomplished, he needed to complete his high-school education.

One night when he was in class, his name was called. "You need to go to the hospital, Bob," his teacher said. "Is your wife expecting a child?"

"She was when I left home!" He exclaimed, jumping up from his desk and sprinting out the door. He arrived at the hospital just a few hours before I was born.

"I always wanted a little girl," Daddy lovingly told me many times. "And I always knew that her name would be Nancy Marie." His words made me feel like a special gift from God just to him.

I can never remember a time that I wondered if Daddy loved me. When I was afraid, he rocked me to sleep. When I was happy, Daddy was happy too. He was always willing to listen when I needed to talk. Some of his answers were not always the response that I wanted to hear, but in his wisdom, he knew what was best for me. When I misbehaved and told him I was sorry, he was always quick to forgive and offer a hug. I never remember going to bed hungry or cold. The house where we lived was comfortable and safe.

Looking back, I am deeply moved by the awesome role model he was. Because of his tremendous love and impact on my life as a father, I've been able to love the eternal, Heavenly Father without reservation.

When I praise His holy name, the sunrise is more beautiful. When I sing songs of joy, echoes of His love linger in my soul. When I give to others, He rewards me with His greatest blessings tenfold. The day that I asked Jesus to come into my heart, He gave me eternal life. And, that is the very best gift I have ever received.

*T*HANKS FOR HAVING ME!

JERRY WAYNE BERNARD

(As told to Muriel Larson)

You saw me before I was born and scheduled each day

of my life before I began to breathe.

PSALM 139:16 TLB

I had just turned twenty-three. As my wife and I were on our knees praying together one night, she reached over and touched me on the arm.

"Jerry Wayne," she said softly, "have you ever prayed for the woman who gave birth to you?"

I looked at Gaylon in surprise. "No, come to think of it, I haven't!"

So I began praying for that nameless girl who had given me life. As I prayed, God laid a burden on my heart for her salvation.

Floyd and Alice Bernard, the wonderful couple who had

"A BABY IS GOD'S OPINION THAT THE WORLD SHOULD GO ON."

Carl Sandburg

adopted me, had wanted children but couldn't have any themselves. They decided to adopt a son. "I want a boy whom God can call to preach," Floyd told friends and relatives.

The Bernards went to a home for unwed mothers, where two newborn boys were available. The nurse put a cute little redheaded baby in Alice's arms and she loved him. Then the nurse brought a little bald-headed thing and laid him in Floyd Bernard's arms.

Floyd looked down at that baby nestling in his arms, then said, "Give that redheaded baby back, Honey. This is the one!"

Through the home, my parents corresponded with the girl who had given birth to me, to let her know how much they loved me and how glad they were that she had given birth to me.

Although my father was strict with me, I never once doubted my parents' love. I in turn loved them dearly and never yearned for any other parents. We had such tremendous love in our little home that I felt especially blessed to have such parents.

When I was seventeen, God answered my parents' prayers and called me to be a minister. On the day after my graduation from a Christian college, I married my sweetheart, Gaylon, and then launched into full-time evangelism.

Not long after I began praying for the salvation of my natural mother, I received a phone call from Gaylon. "Honey, brace yourself," she said. "Your dad just died of a heart attack."

The news pierced my heart. My legs turned to jelly, and I collapsed to my knees, weeping for that dear humble man of God.

I flew back to Texas to be with my mother. After the funeral we went through papers to find out what insurance my dad had. I came across an old envelope. Opening it carefully, I found inside the birth certificate of a boy who had been born on my birth date—Joe Ed Middleton. His mother's name was given: Robbie Lee Middleton.

"Mother, what's this?" I asked, handing the paper to her.

"That's your original birth certificate," she said.

Well, I thought later, *I guess God wants me to know Robbie Lee's name so that I can better pray for her.*

When I looked at my birth certificate again, I saw a town listed next to Robbie Lee's name: Guyon, Texas. I couldn't find it on the map.

One day, however, I found an older map of Texas in an antique shop. The name "Guyon" virtually leaped out at me. I decided to drive there to find out where Robbie Lee was and hopefully send a minister friend to share the gospel with her.

Guyon was a ghost town. As I walked the deserted main street, looking at broken store windows, I felt the desolation of the place. Then suddenly I saw a woman approaching me, and I called out to greet her.

This proved to be the only time she had come back to Guyon since she had left many years ago, and her visit would only be a short fifteen minutes before her husband came to pick her up. I asked her if she had known a girl named Robbie Lee Middleton.

"I went to school with her," the woman answered. She knew where my natural mother lived and how I could get in touch with her!

Stunned at this amazing coincidence, I thought, *God has got to be in this!*

When I got home, I obtained Robbie Lee's phone number. All I had in mind was to tell her that I was a preacher and to share how God had blessed my life.

She actually answered the phone herself—and amazingly she knew immediately that I was her son. "We've been searching for you for fifteen years!" she cried. She told me that she had run away to get married when she was sixteen, but her father had annulled the marriage before learning she was pregnant.

That weekend Gaylon and I went to visit my natural mother and other relatives. What a shock I had as they poured out of the house to greet me—a whole bunch of strangers who looked just like me! What a thrilling reunion! I invited them to come visit us the following weekend.

Several days later I visited the home for unwed mothers to

tell them what had happened. They showed me the record of my birth and their specially recorded prayer request for me: It was that God would call me to preach!

That Saturday night my new family heard me share the gospel at a youth rally. The next morning when the invitation to receive Christ was given, my mother and sisters came down the aisle to get saved. Falling on my knees, I thanked God for answering my seemingly impossible prayers.

I'm so thankful that my natural mother brought me into the world. I'm thankful that in those days abortion wasn't an easy or acceptable practice, or my life might have been snuffed out. I never would have been blessed with the joy of singing and ministering the love of God to others by sharing His message throughout the world at revivals, crusades—and even at a Presidential Prayer Breakfast.

Who knows what great purpose God may have for a person's life? The possibilities are endless.

$\mathcal{F}$IRMLY PLANTED

TRIPP CURTIS

He will be like a tree planted by the water....

JEREMIAH 17:8 NIV

"A man's gotta do what a man's gotta do," I grumbled as I loaded my well-worn climbing saddle and chainsaw into the trunk of our car.

"I hope this old saw still has some life in it." It had been years since I'd used it. Even though I'd done tree work in my late teens, I'd gladly left it in my twenties to join the Coast Guard. As a navigator on a ship sailing from San Francisco to Alaska, I'd found the fulfillment of my boyhood dreams, spun from tales of *Horatio Hornblower* and other adventures of men at sea.

How lucky I was to live the life I'd always dreamed of!

And now how far I'd fallen! Tree work seemed so lowly, made me too aware of my lack of a college education. After years of being in uniform, finding my identity through my

"FAMILY FACES
ARE LIKE
MAGIC
MIRRORS.
LOOKING AT
PEOPLE WHO
BELONG
TO US, WE
SEE THE PAST,
PRESENT,
AND FUTURE.
WE MAKE
DISCOVERIES
ABOUT
OURSELVES."

Gail Lumet Buckley

association with the sea, I suddenly felt like nobody at all.

Except that now I was a husband and a father. Five months earlier, I'd married the woman of my dreams. Well, the woman of my dreams along with her two children. Samantha and Jasmine, thirteen and six, were part of the wedding package, but I never knew for sure if I would have fallen so much in love with Barbara without them. At twenty-seven, I felt ready for responsibility, confident that I could be a good provider, and even more excited to find out another new baby was on the way.

By the time I met Barbara, I had fulfilled my Coast Guard enlistment and was working as operations manager for a tug and barge company on the San Francisco Bay. Financially secure, I realized only after the wedding that my job was in other ways incompatible with the lifestyle of a family—at least the kind of family Barbara had in mind.

Our newly-wedded bliss was soon disrupted by frequent three A.M. emergency calls, causing me to bolt out of bed, jump into my foul-weather gear, and disappear into the night. I'd get so caught up in the drama of cleaning up an oil spill or repairing a blown engine, I'd completely forget to call home. When I'd finally drag my exhausted body home forty-eight or seventy-two hours later, I seldom received the kind of welcome I wanted.

Once Barbara was so mad she wouldn't even let me sleep until we'd "talked it out." I refused and checked into a hotel instead, where I slept for a couple of days, and then took a few more while I weighed what really mattered to me.

No matter whether I needed my family or not, I decided, they certainly needed me more than what I'd been giving. Reluctantly, I gave my notice at my job.

But when I quit my job, I never intended to quit the sea. Perhaps I hoped to buy my own tugboat, be my own boss, and thus have more control over my time. But the banks weren't cooperating. After all, we were just a one-car family with a rented house and no collateral. And now with no income, we faced the prospect of losing what little we had.

And so it had come to this—that I would have to fall back on my tree skills, working by the hour to feed my family. Thank God I had hung onto my chainsaw and climbing saddle! At least we could get by for a few days while I figured out what to do next.

Days turned into weeks. When I ran out of acquaintances to work for, I placed a small ad to find new customers. Barbara began answering calls and scheduling estimates. I learned to meet customers, bid jobs, and face rejection. I hoped I wouldn't be doing this much longer.

Weeks turned into months. I bought a truck, hired an assistant. But when Barbara suggested getting some work proposals printed up, I balked. After all, this was only temporary, and I didn't want to invest in anything I couldn't get rid of easily.

As I worked on trees each day, I dreamed of the sea, especially as the summer began to simmer. I began to simmer too. Our baby was due the next month, and while Barbara was feeling content that I was home every night, I was feeling resentful and full of despair.

One day my assistant called in sick. That left me with an aching arm and a big job to do alone. I was working on the street where I grew up, in Mr. Sanor's backyard, trimming back a high and unruly hedge. The work was not going well because the lever on my pole pruner kept sticking. I was getting hotter, sweatier, dirtier, and crankier by the minute. Things just weren't going my way, not only with this job but throughout my entire life. As my frustration mounted, I found myself arguing with God: *I just don't understand! Why can't I get back to the sea? Am I supposed to be stuck in these trees for the rest of my life?*

Suddenly, as though I had reached the eye of the hurricane, my whirlwind of emotions came to rest. I was filled with peace. Perhaps it was because I had asked a direct question that I heard an answer. Suddenly I was filled with assurance and a sense of purpose. Serving others and taking care of God's creation was to be my calling. What better way to be there for my wife and children, as well as to contribute to my community!

I will never forget coming home and wrapping Barbara, and our soon-to-be-born son, in my arms.

"I'm home, honey," I said.

"I can see that," she said, puzzled by my tone.

"No, I mean, I'm *really* home," and I tried to explain the change in me, how my heart had finally caught up with the new direction my life had taken, how ready I was to finally embrace the calling I'd been unable to hear.

The next week, I was working for an Irish lady who brought out a cup of coffee and said in a thick brogue, "You know, they really ought to call you *Mr. Trees*." When I told Barbara, she agreed wholeheartedly, and promptly ordered business cards boasting our new company's name. And a month later our first son, Joshua, was born.

After that, life just hurtled along—more employees, more equipment, more customers—and more kids. Now, twenty years later, "Mr. Trees" is consistently voted the best tree service in our county, serving 1,000 people a year and providing work for twenty-five employees. Barbara and I now have twelve children—through both birth and adoption—and eight grandchildren.

But through it all, I've never forgotten that moment when God placed a peace in my heart about my true calling. As Mr. Trees, my roots have been firmly planted.

$\mathcal{F}$ROM GRIEF TO GIFTS

JOE TYE

Yea, though I walk through the valley of the

shadow of death, I will fear no evil.

PSALM 23:4

I am often privileged to speak with members of various support groups. I talk about finding the courage and strength to cope with adversity and the negative emotions that often come in its wake. Before each meeting, I visualize myself struggling with whatever problem brought that particular group together: cancer, head injuries, living alone, weight problems, addictions; you name the problem—there's a support group for it.

The first of the Twelve Core Action Values of the *Never Fear, Never Quit* personal leadership effectiveness curriculum is *Authenticity;* and how could I possibly be authentic as a speaker if I couldn't at least imagine myself in the shoes, or in the wheelchairs, of my listeners?

Then I was invited to spend an evening with Compassionate Friends. They are a support group for parents who have lost children. I couldn't imagine myself handling that particular tragedy with courage and perseverance, and I didn't even want to try for fear that the mental image might somehow influence events in the real world. The loss of a child is the one tragedy for which I could never be prepared and with which I do not believe I could cope.

But I had agreed to attend so, with great trepidation, when the appointed evening arrived I turned off the lights and headed for the door. On my way out of the office, my eye was caught by a little Guardian Angel doll that a friend had made out of corn silk. Not knowing for sure what I would do with her, I picked up the doll and took it with me.

There were about fifty people seated in a circle in the church basement that evening. As was their custom, they began the meeting with a prayer, and then went around the room, each telling something about the loss of their child. There were many tears and many hugs, and I was relieved to realize that *this* was the main event; my remarks would actually be anticlimactic.

The circle of introductions finally made it around to the couple just to my right. Their child had very recently passed away, and this was their first meeting. It was brutally evident that they had not even begun to cope with the devastating shock—they didn't believe they would ever again crawl out from under the glacier of grief that had suddenly permeated their lives.

For one of the few times in my life, I was at a loss for words—a strange state of affairs for a professional speaker! I felt that anything I might say would only diminish the gravity of the moment. All I could think of to do was give the grieving couple the Guardian Angel doll I'd picked up, seemingly as an afterthought, as I'd left my office.

Then something miraculous began to happen. After several very long moments of silence, one of the Compassionate Friends said something like this: I know it's impossible for you to see anything good ever coming out of such an incomprehensible tragedy, and it might seem pretty callous of me to suggest that it could. But let me share this with you: While the death of my child was the most horrible experience of my life, I am a much better parent for my other children than I would have been had that tragedy not happened. My priorities were totally rearranged as a result of realizing the value of what I'd lost.

After a few more moments, another Compassionate Friend spoke up, commenting on how after the loss of her child, she was much more aware of the fleeting fragility of life, and of the precious beauty of each passing moment. Today she could find humor in the little annoyances that would once have ruined her day because they were so trivial next to the real loss she now understood. She wished it hadn't been so, she added, but the death of her child had helped her be more awake, more alive.

Another Compassionate Friend shared that she was writing a book about how to prevent the kind of accident that had claimed her own child's life. She wanted to do anything in her power to prevent other parents from experiencing the tragedy that had shattered her life. The writing was also a way of rebuilding her life, and of creating an enduring legacy to the memory of her child.

One by one, the Compassionate Friends offered the newly-bereaved couple hope. One by one, they took the grief in their hearts and transformed it into a gift for this couple—the Gift of Hope.

After my remarks, the evening ended with the sharing of coffee and cookies, and with hugs and private words of condolence for the new couple. I commented that I hoped they could find a suitable place for the little doll I'd given them; the mother looked at me with a sort of fierce determination and replied, "It's not a *doll*—it's a Guardian Angel!" I felt like someone who had just heard the first springtime cracking of the ice sheet on a river after a long hard winter.

It is natural, inevitable, and even healthy to experience grief after a tragic loss. As Freud once pointed out, failure to acknowledge and honor grief up-front is likely to result in depression later. At some point, however, a decision must be made between taking up permanent residence in the valley of the shadow of death, or following the Compassionate Friends and moving on.

One of the most effective ways of moving on, it seems to me, is by transforming your grief into someone else's gift. With the wisdom endowed by your grief, can you help someone else move from anger and bitterness about the years they've lost toward gratitude for the years with which they were blessed? Can you show someone who is trapped in the darkness a path that leads toward the light? Can you sympathize with their despair and, at the same time, give them hope?

What gift could be more precious than the comfort of a loving guide? What legacy could be more enduring than to plant the seeds of hope in a grief-stricken heart? What transformation could be more healing than turning your grief into someone else's gift?

$\mathcal{H}$OME FOR CHRISTMAS

RICHARD C. STARGEL

(With Gloria Cassity Stargel)

They cried out to the Lord in their trouble,

and he delivered them out of their distresses.

PSALM 107:6 NKJV

It is 5 o'clock in the afternoon on the 27th of December. At the Dallas/Fort Worth Airport, the terminal teems with edgy travelers studying their watches. Our little family of three maneuvers past computer screens filled with notices of cancelled and delayed flights. "That winter storm on the East Coast is causing havoc with air travel *everywhere*," I moan.

The public address system keeps up a steady stream of announcements in Spanish, then English. Harried agents try to cope with countless questions whose answers keep changing. We reach Gate 8. "Flight 832 to Atlanta is on schedule for a 6:43 departure," I read out loud. "What a relief!" For a few moments, I allow "visions of sugarplums" to dance in my head. Only this time, it's Mom's roasted turkey and cornbread stuffing.

"I hope we make it," my wife, Lisa, says, setting our little nine-month-old Richard down to play with his toys. "I know your parents want to see Richard enjoy his first Christmas."

"Oh, yes," I answer. "Too bad I had to work Christmas day." In my mind, I picture Mom and Dad, waiting to celebrate Christmas until the family could be together, a practice they'd started while I was on active duty with the Marine Corps. "My mother is like a mama cat with her brood of kittens," I tell Lisa, "fully content only when we are safely gathered close by."

"Why don't you call them and check on the weather in Georgia?" Lisa asks. It's hard to realize that icy conditions are paralyzing everything there, while out here we had just ridden past mesquite trees with brilliant sunshine glancing off their bare limbs.

In a few minutes, I'm back. "Mom says it's getting worse. Freezing rain and sleet are making driving hazardous. Hartsfield International reports dense fog plus air traffic already backed up due to blizzards in the northeast."

"On top of the threatening weather," Lisa adds, "it was a bit unnerving to see that television report just before coming out to the airport."

"About the unscheduled landing here this afternoon?" I

silently recall the facts: *The airline jet flying from Seattle to Atlanta made an unscheduled landing due to problems with its hydraulic system used to steer the craft on the ground.*

"I'd just as soon not be reminded before we fly off into the wild blue yonder that airplanes have problems." Lisa manages a grin.

"The good news is," I reassure her, "all 228 passengers came away unharmed." I send up a hasty prayer, *Lord, please give us a safe trip home.*

As time drags on, Richard gets restless. "Lisa, if you'll stay with the bags, I'll walk him around awhile." The two of us reach Gate 15 where I chance to hear a red-coated airline employee speak with a tone of concern into his walkie-talkie: "Flight 832 has been cancelled."

My ears snap to attention. "Did you just say Flight 832 has been cancelled? That's my flight!"

"Yes," he replies. "That plane is being held at its departure point. If you want to get to Atlanta tonight, you'd better get on *this* one in a hurry. Air traffic at Hartsfield is so snarled, we have only a fifteen-minute window to get in there."

With that, Richard and I do an about-face and sprint off down the concourse to gather up Lisa and our gear. We hustle back to Gate 15. Flight attendants double as gate attendants. "It's open seating," they say as they rush us aboard. Inside the cavernous aircraft, we—along with a handful of other passengers—take our pick of seats. Within minutes, the plane pushes back from the gate.

We're airborne when we hear a flight attendant mention the word "Seattle." Lisa and I exchange startled looks that say, *Uh, oh! We're on the 767 that landed at Dallas this afternoon due to mechanical problems!* Of course, common sense tells me the airline would not let the plane fly if it were not ready. Still…Dear Lord, protect us, I pray.

My concern travels to Georgia. *I'm sure our family has learned about our cancelled flight. They're probably wondering where we are and why we aren't calling.* I picture the house, decorated from top to bottom. And on the coffee table, in its traditional place of honor, is our unique nativity scene—unique because it consists of only two figures. The Bible is opened to the Christmas story in Luke chapter 2. Just in front of that, there is a small ceramic figure of the Christ Child. Watching over Him—lovingly, prayerfully—is His mother.

By now, my mother is peering out the window for the hundredth time, worrying about the weather. And praying we'll get a flight out and a safe trip home. *Please, Lord….*

About 10 o'clock, aboard the 767, the "Fasten Seatbelts" lights flash on. The captain announces, "We're making our final approach into Hartsfield." I look out the window. Fog is so thick our landing lights bounce back at us off the mist. A runway is nowhere to be seen. I pray the hydraulic system is in good working order, then listen for the lowering of landing gear. *Thump. Groan. Grind.* Perfectly normal sounds, I tell myself. But I admit that my breath catches as the wheels impact the runway. They hold. Whew! *Thank You, Lord.*

We spill out into the terminal at Hartsfield International and locate a pay phone to call home. "Mom?"

"Where *are* you?" she asks, sounding relieved to hear my voice. "Back at your apartment in Texas?"

"No, ma'am, we're at the Atlanta airport."

"But you can't be!" Mom exclaims. "We've talked with the Airline several times. There was not another flight coming in tonight! How in the world did you get here—on a *phantom flight?*"

"You're not going to believe it," I say, somewhat in awe myself. "I'll tell you the whole story when we get home."

We collect our rental car and cautiously head north on I-85 for the fifty-mile drive to Gainesville. In his car seat, travel-weary Richard falls sound asleep. Picking our way through thick fog and treacherous black ice on the highway, I hear the radio announcer report road closings and power outages and poor visibility. On the open road, our headlights occasionally pierce the grayness to reveal tall, skinny pine trees bending almost to the ground, their needles coated with ice.

At long last, we're almost home, and I replay in my mind the events of the past several hours. "You know, Lisa," my voice breaks the silence, "if I hadn't been walking Richard we wouldn't have caught that plane. We'd still be in Texas."

"And Richard would be terribly out-of-sorts by now," she adds.

"Yes. And think how, when we needed a plane to Atlanta, one was sitting there—completely unplanned—ready to take off. And an almost private, *gigantic plane,* at that!"

"Besides," I go on, "our original flight would have been in a much smaller plane, possibly ill-equipped to land under such adverse weather conditions. *This* one carried all the latest sophisticated equipment!"

"Rick," Lisa responds, "I think we just received a very special Christmas gift—maybe even a miracle!"

"I think you're right."

At 12:45 in the morning, tired but safe, we pull into the driveway. All lights of the house are on—both outside and inside. The front door swings open and out rush Mom, Dad, and my brother, Randy, along with the aroma of holiday spices, baking turkey, and burning logs in the fireplace.

In the living room, we become a Christmas-card scene with more hugs and laughter, a roaring fire, bright, twinkling lights on the tree, and tinkling bells playing *Silent Night, Holy Night.*

And on the coffee table, the tiny ceramic figure of Mary beams down on her babe in the manger. *Yes, it is good to be home!*

Thank You, Jesus, I say silently from my heart. I join the others around the tree, and then do an about-face toward the little nativity scene. *"Oh, and Sir,"* I whisper, *"HAPPY BIRTHDAY!"*

$\mathcal{T}$HE BANNER OF LOVE

NANCY GIBBS

His banner over me is love.

SONG OF SONGS 2:4 NIV

Those were some of the hardest days of my life. In his early sixties, my father's personality changed for the worse. We had gradually noticed many changes since he retired at fifty-five. He had big plans for his retirement years that never worked out. His temper raged and paranoia plagued him. Daddy lashed out at everyone, except me. And soon our family members discovered that I was the only one who could do anything with him.

Therefore, on a sorrowful Sunday afternoon, I was the one who was forced to admit him into the hospital, where he would be treated for depression. At the same time, the doctors would try to find a way to stop the progression of Parkinson's disease. When I left him there that day, I sobbed the entire way home.

Until that day, I never realized how badly a broken heart

could hurt. We discovered that the medication for his illness was causing both the paranoia and the violent episodes he experienced. But when the medication was discontinued, the Parkinson's disease progressed rapidly.

A few weeks later, our family had to make the decision to admit Daddy into a nursing home. He needed round-the-clock medical care. My heart ached even worse that night than the day I had taken him to the hospital. It all seemed so final.

I cried myself to sleep that night and woke up the next morning feeling like I had let Daddy down. The doctors all told me that there was nothing I could do to help him, but I hated leaving him in that nursing home room. I wanted desperately for him to know how much I loved him. But how could I convince him of my love after leaving him in such a cold and dreary place? During my quiet time that morning, God spoke to my heart and gave me an idea.

I printed a banner with a cupid at each end holding a scroll. On the scroll I printed these words, "I Love You." I took it to the nursing home, showed it to Daddy, and asked him to read it. I hung it on the wall so he could see it from his bed.

"When you're here alone, Daddy, and wonder if anybody loves you, just read this banner, and remember how much *I* love you," I said. Daddy smiled and said he would.

For four long years the sign hung in Daddy's room. During

that time, Daddy forgot who I was, even though I visited several times each week. He knew he loved me, however, and one day he even asked me to marry him. I smiled and accepted.

Many times, I have wondered how many lonely times Daddy read the poster that I made for him. I hoped and prayed that he knew the words were true.

Finally, one February morning, Daddy went to be with the Lord. He escaped his frail body and shattered mind. He was made whole in Heaven that day. But my grieving heart was fractured. I needed to hold him. I wanted to dance with him. But mostly, I wanted him to say, "I love you!" just one more time.

That afternoon I walked into the empty nursing home room to pack up his few belongings. I took the sign off the wall, carefully folded it up and took it home with me. I hung it on the wall of my study.

During a difficult time a few weeks later, I fell asleep in the chair facing the sign. I awoke in the middle of the night, and the first vision I saw was the banner of love that I had made some four years earlier. God knew that at that time I needed a sign myself. The light from the other room illuminated the words.

Little did I know the day that I made the sign that it would get me through many trying days, weeks, months, and years after Daddy died. It has been almost another four years and the sign continues to hang in my study. When the grief over losing him almost becomes unbearable, I glance at the banner.

Daddy may be gone, but the simple banner gives me a renewed hope for the future. I know that one day we will be together again in Heaven. There, we won't need a sign to say "I love you." We will be able to say it again, face-to-face and heart-to-heart, anytime we wish. And in that place, we will never have to say good-bye again.

LOCKING UP FOR THE NIGHT

ROBIN BAYNE

As a father pities his children, so the Lord pities those who fear Him.

PSALM 103:13 NKJV

We were playing Beauty Shop, a favorite game of my little sister, our best friend, Colleen, and mine. My mother was downstairs helping her friend, "Aunt Kathy," straighten the house for a tour of prospective buyers who were on their way with a real estate agent.

We were on the second floor of the Cape Cod style house, where Colleen's bedroom and a guest room sat on either side of the hall bathroom.

"You kids keep that room straight up there," Aunt Kathy yelled up the stairs. The smell of pine cleaner and a pie baking in the oven drifted upward.

"We will," we promised, lining up dolls in order for us to

work on their hair.

"We should take each one to the bathroom," I suggested, "so we can wash their hair in the sink." It was agreed, and we proceeded to beautify the inanimate population of Colleen's toy chest. We were all elementary-school age, but I was the oldest and got to be the owner of the beauty shop and give the orders. When we were done, I took a towel and wiped out the porcelain sink, recalling the need to clean as we went. Then, as a good shop owner would do, I flicked the light switch off, pressed the lock button in the door handle, and pulled it closed behind me.

Click.

As I heard the click I realized my mistake. There was no key! There was no way to unlock the door from the hallway side. There was a small hole in the doorknob, so much as I dreaded it, I had to go get my mother and admit what I'd done. They were going to kill me!

Although neither Mom nor Aunt Kathy seemed to care that it was an accident, they did stay rather calm through the process of poking sharp objects into the handle, trying to spring the lock button on the other side. Nothing they tried worked. Meanwhile, I stood around shifting from one foot to the other, dreading the lecture and punishment to come. Even if that didn't occur, the cold shoulders were hard enough to bear. My stomach burned with acidic fear. Why, oh why, had I locked that door?

"The real estate lady is here," Colleen called from downstairs. She'd followed my mother down as she went to call my father, who was a mechanic and worked nearby. Aunt Kathy showed the downstairs to the people and within a few minutes, Dad arrived. He worked on the door from the hall, tried several things, and grunted a few times, just shaking his head at me. He said nothing, though, as was his usual way. His manner was that of a quiet man, a decent and kind man.

Finally, he decided he had to get in from the outside, so he climbed to the roof and made his way around to the little bathroom window, and somehow squeezed inside. I said a little prayer for his safety and for my own, once he unlocked the door. We had held our breath as he inched across, and now relaxed as he disappeared into the small opening. A few seconds later, the lock popped and the door swung open into the hall.

Mom peered inside, obviously expecting a mess, but nodded as if pleased. The pressure was relieved, but I still feared the lecture to come. I followed Dad outside, planning to ride home with him, since it was too late in the afternoon for him to go back to work.

"Daddy, we were just playing Beauty Shop. Please don't be mad, but I cleaned the sink and everything. We were done for the day, so I locked the door, just like you and Mom would. I'm sorry Aunt Kathy was so mad at us." I sighed. "Well, so mad at *me*."

We got into his car, and I sat very straight, waiting for the axe to fall. Finally he looked at me and to my surprise, grinned from ear to ear. Had he thought this was funny?

"Well," he said, turning the key in the ignition. "At least you've learned to lock up when you leave!"

I smiled over at Dad, as if we had a little secret. *What a cool father,* I thought. *Everyone should have one like him.*

That was the last I heard about the incident, but it was always remembered. I still thank God for my wonderful father every chance I get. Even when I lock up for the night.

$\mathcal{T}$HE THIRD MIRACLE

LIANA METAL

Jesus looked at them and said, "With man this is impossible,

but not with God; all things are possible with God."

MARK 10:27 NIV

Victoria slammed the door behind her.

"I don't want to see you again," she shouted back.

She walked fast and nervously towards her car, in the front drive of their house.

Kevin has ruined my life, she thought once more. *But I'll get my revenge. I owe it to myself!*

She got into her car, accelerated, and drove away.

Kevin sat in an armchair, talking excitedly on the phone.

"She's driving me crazy! She's absolutely insane! I don't know what to do with her," he confessed to his closest friend, Peter.

Their marriage had been on the rocks for quite some time.

Victoria accused Kevin, and Kevin accused Victoria. And their twin children, Chris and Elena, accused them both.

"Something must be done," Chris told his sister one day. "This situation can't go on!"

"I agree," Elena replied. "But what can we do?"

Actually, they had tried everything. Not even Elena's ill health could stop them from getting a divorce.

"Think of the twins," Victoria's sister advised her. "Elena needs you...her health could be at risk anytime. You know that, don't you?"

"That's another problem that, unfortunately, cannot be solved. And it has nothing to do with our relationship," Victoria would say.

But in her heart, she knew that Elena was in danger. She suffered from acute anemia and needed monthly blood transfusions. Both of them were aware of the fact that she might lose the battle with life at any time, and as she reached her late teens, the risk was increasing. Fortunately her twin brother, Chris, was normal. Victoria prayed for her daughter every day and hoped that God would keep her alive for a long time. But as Elena's health was so fragile, she needed a quiet family life and to feel safe and loved.

"Let's cancel the divorce procedure," Kevin suggested one day. "It's the best for all of us. Why go to extremes?"

Victoria knew that they had both overreacted, but she did not want to retreat. She was stubborn and set in her ways.

"No way," she plainly said. Kevin knew she meant it. Victoria had made her plans, but God had His own plans, as well.

"I'm getting married," Elena announced one evening.

Victoria called Kevin at once. They had to talk. For Elena's sake, they met and tried to solve their daughter's problem.

"We have to ask her doctor," Kevin suggested. "Maybe it's dangerous…in case she decides to have a family…in her condition."

Victoria agreed. She was concerned about her daughter. The doctor told them that as Elena's health was steady, she could go ahead with her plans. At nineteen, Elena got married to her high-school sweetheart, John, and settled into a new house next door to John's parents. After the wedding, Victoria moved into an apartment of her own, and tried to find a job. Kevin did not press her. He was already fed up with her attitude.

One day, Elena called her mom.

"Good news, Mom! I'm going to be a mom myself!"

Victoria was amazed. However, she was scared as well.

"Can she have children? Isn't it dangerous in her condition?" she asked the doctor.

But the doctor was optimistic.

"She'll survive, don't worry, and she'll have a beautiful baby," he assured her.

"What about the baby? Will it be healthy?" Kevin asked the doctor when he heard the news.

The doctor assured him that nothing bad would happen to mother or baby, and that they shouldn't worry. "I'll keep an eye on her on a daily basis. She'll be fine," he said.

Victoria and Kevin started talking again. They were both concerned about Elena. Moreover, Victoria's first job had been a disaster, and Kevin offered to support her financially. She pushed her pride aside and accepted. She was already feeling insecure and lonely but she did not want to admit it.

"You're going to be a grandma of twins," Elena announced one day. "Can you believe it? I'm gonna have twins!" She was overjoyed, but a bit scared.

Victoria and Kevin decided to meet for dinner that evening.

"God help her," Kevin said. "She's so tiny and fragile, and she's going to have twins!"

"This is a miracle, Kevin," Victoria replied. "It's a miracle she's lived till today, and this is another miracle. It's never crossed my mind that Elena will make us grandparents, let alone have twins!"

"It runs in the family," Kevin said and smiled.

Victoria smiled back for the first time in a long time.

Somehow this evening was very special and enjoyable as well.

That night Victoria made up her mind.

I'll go back home if he asks me to, she thought.

But Kevin was hesitant.

"Try once more," his close friend Peter encouraged him. "Now is the perfect time to make up!"

"I'm not sure if I can go through the same situation all over again," Kevin replied. "I need time to think."

Meanwhile, Elena's twins were due any day.

"They're due next week," Elena told her mom. "Will you come to my place to help? I need you!"

Victoria moved into Elena's house for a while. The twins were delivered by caesarian section, and both of them were healthy. Elena was also in good condition, but she needed to be taken care of for some time. Victoria became a devoted nurse and mother, but when two weeks had passed, she decided it was high time she left Elena's family on her own.

When she returned to her own apartment, it felt so lonely that she could no longer stand it. She decided to call Kevin.

"How about sharing our house?" she suggested hesitantly. "If you don't mind, of course. I don't feel safe in that apartment."

Kevin accepted.

"On one condition, though," he said. "We are friends,

nothing more. I can't promise you anything right now. Let's just take it step by step."

"Okay," Victoria consented, "let's try becoming friends first."

Their divorce had already been finalized, but this fact didn't hold them back.

"God has offered our daughter a normal life with a family and children of her own," Victoria said one day. "Isn't it a pity to be apart? Grandparents should help their grandchildren… together."

"I'm glad you can see that," Kevin said. "God's given us a great gift, so we mustn't spoil it."

And their reunion became the third miracle in their family.

Who can deny the power of God?

*O*N BENDED KNEE

CAROL TERMIN

Wives, submit yourselves to your own husbands, as unto the Lord...

Husbands, love your wives, even as Christ loved also the church,

and gave himself for it.

EPHESIANS 5:22,25

"CHAINS DO
NOT HOLD A
MARRIAGE
TOGETHER. IT
IS THREADS,
HUNDREDS
OF TINY
THREADS,
WHICH SEW
PEOPLE
TOGETHER
THROUGH
THE YEARS."

Simone Signoret

I picked up my husband's jeans to put them in the laundry, and the torn knee in the pant leg brought back clear memories of our years together, especially his role as a father. When I first met my husband, he was on bended knee at his car, checking a pipe. I have seen him that way many times since. And so I honor the man in my life.

He learned how to pray, as his mother and father trained him in faith and throughout his life, he would "talk it over" with God on bended knee.

He stooped to catch a frog, to find what it was all about. He "drove" toy trucks and cars and dreamed of future races. He watched a spider weave a web that caught a fly and got a close-up look, on bended knee.

He moistened his hands with spit and tightened the bolts on his bike. He tried to look professional, mitt in hand, as he bowed to catch what the batter missed on bended knee.

He changed his first tire. He installed the "latest" in pipes to his first car and searched beneath it when he lost the keys, on bended knee.

He promised her everything when he proposed to his girl, in marriage on bended knee.

He constructed the new bike that he would place under the Christmas tree. He taught his children to hit their first ball at "their level." And he listened to their prayers at night, right alongside them, on bended knee.

He placed the flowers on the grave, to honor his loved one, and gently pulled the weeds from the headstone on bended knee.

And now that the children are grown, he is still on his knees, praying for their protection. And still promising her everything.

And with love and admiration in my heart, I gently patch the hole in the knee of his pant leg and wash the jeans, of a man who humbly crawled to greatness, on bended knee.

WINNERS AND LOSERS

DAVID FLANAGAN

Better a dry crust with peace and quiet than

a house full of feasting, with strife.

PROVERBS 17:1 NIV

Not long ago my teenage son and I were arguing and as he walked away he muttered under his breath, "Dad, you're a jobless loser." The words were muffled but they reverberated as though they had been shouted from the highest mountaintop. I didn't say a word to my son because I didn't quite know exactly how to respond. I was certain that my son's words didn't reflect his true feelings toward me, but just the same they wounded as surely as though a knife had been plunged through my heart.

My wife and sons have been justifiably worried about our future since I lost my job in November. *Maybe he's right,* I thought, *after all I am jobless!* Like many, the economy had taken its toll on my career.

A short time later my trance was disturbed when my young tormentor approached me and apologized, saying "Dad, you may be jobless but you're not a loser."

Recently, I had been unjustly laid off from my job and since then had tried unsuccessfully to land another full-time job in the nebulous field of community and government relations.

Since that time I have followed the path that most traverse when abruptly faced with unemployment. Revamping the resume, signing up for unemployment benefits, upgrading the computer, submitting your name to myriad recruiters, and harassing acquaintances with whom you had lost touch to let them know of your availability.

Since the argument with my son, I have repeatedly asked myself whether he was right and wondered if perhaps I am a "loser." Thinking back over the career and life choices I have made, second-guessing each decision as if I could make it again.

I have thought about what it truly means to be a success and how one distinguishes between being a winner or a loser. I began to think of the friends I'd had when I was a kid. Growing up in the projects in the 1960s meant that at any given moment you had the chance to hang around with literally hundreds of kids. As I reflected upon my past I jotted down the names of the dozen or so kids who came to mind and listed their accomplishments next to their name. Of that group, I know that at least five of them have committed murder, eight have served time in various prisons, most have abused alcohol and drugs, and some never escaped the projects.

Thirty-five or so years ago my friends and I were my son's age but we were different in so very many ways. Some of us were dependent upon welfare, others were illegitimate, most were living in homes without love, fathers, or role models. Many awoke each morning to alcohol abuse and domestic violence and went to bed each evening praying that the next day would be better than the last. *How,* I wondered, *have my friends fared in life? How might their lives have been different if their environment had been more stable?*

As I reflect on these things I take little comfort in thinking about the tragic lives my friends have endured compared to my own. However, it causes me to think about why I was allowed to escape from welfare and the projects, avoid jail and drug abuse, purchase my own home, attend college and grad school, and have a reasonably successful career. Given my *current* career situation, I suppose one could conceivably consider me a loser.

But then again, perhaps my son was right—I may be jobless but I have a family who loves me and that makes me a winner in the end.

I FOUND HOPE

KEVIN WHITWORTH

Christin you, the hope of glory.

COLOSSIANS 1:27

I found hope.

I was despondent. I needed a change. Nothing I did was working. I tried to ignore God, but I couldn't resist Him any longer. So with tears in my eyes, I made my way down the aisle and accepted Jesus as my Savior. This may sound like "common fare" to some people, but my conversion was anything but standard.

My life was in a shambles because of my alcohol and drug addictions. My actions tore my family asunder. Too many of my meals came from a twelve-ounce can. Even worse, I skipped many meals in favor of snorting crystal meth up my nose. My friends were the worst—at best. I tried to depend on myself—instead, I was desperately dependent on drugs.

I was at church, but only because my wife and I were beginning marriage counseling. A trust had long ago been broken and my wife wouldn't take me back unless I went to counseling with her, so I did. I was attending counseling out of obligation. But unexpectedly something happened—I began to truly change. It was a long journey, yet God touched my life answering my parent's prayers. Prayers they had spoken for more than ten years.

I became a child of God, and I was loving it. I felt new and clean, and I knew God wanted me to live a different life. But I also knew that I was not strong enough to hang out with my old friends who were still living the same old life.

Desperate to make a new start, my family and I moved 2000 miles from Missouri to the great northwest. I had been in that part of the country before, and I assured my wife that I could find a job and we would live happily ever after. You can imagine our shock when we arrived in Portland, Oregon, to a significantly higher cost of living than we could have ever imagined. And if that weren't bad enough, because of my credit history we couldn't even secure an apartment.

To make matters worse I only had two more checks from my previous employer, which to our horror, did not arrive.

My family had stayed in motels for nearly a month, and we were running low on money. I had promised my kids I would take them camping, and I thought this would be the most logical time to do it. So with precious little money, my family and I loaded up the van and headed for the great outdoors. People told me how beautiful it was on the Washington side of the Columbia River Gorge, so naively we went there. I say "naively" because we were unaware of the weather patterns. We came to a beautiful State Park that also had a campground, and we set up camp there.

I had thought that camping would save us money, and I could drive back and forth to the city to look for a job and check the mail for the paychecks. While this seemed like a good idea at the time, it didn't work out the way we had hoped. We stayed the maximum number of days plus one and were forced to move on. I'd heard that in the national forest you could camp for free—which by now was all we could afford. We settled down and made camp there.

The checks finally came, but we did not move back into town again. We opted to stay in the woods—unaware of the rainy season that was approaching. I didn't know that it rained a hundred inches annually right where we were camping. And, the rain came! It rained every day for over a month—the sun never shined, our things got wet, and many of our things were ruined. I still didn't have a job, and I began to think that God was punishing me, or even worse, that maybe He'd given up on me. In frustration and anger I ripped our tent into shreds and threw it in the campfire.

Now we didn't even have a shelter from the rain. My wife and I finally decided to take the resources we had left and send the kids back to Missouri. It felt as if our situation was hopeless.

My wife and I did not know what else to do, and so we began to pray. We asked God for help. And then things started happening so fast we could hardly keep up with them. God gave me a good job about five miles from where we were camping. This meant I no longer had to drive the seventy-plus miles to Portland for work at the daily temporary services. The first day on the job I received a raise. Then to my amazement, after just working three days, one of the workers let my wife and me stay in his trailer for free.

God wasn't finished. As we were staying in the trailer, another worker came to me and asked whether I was looking for a place to live. We were able to work out a fair deal for more permanent housing. I began to realize that God had not run out on me after all—I had just been ignoring the most powerful resource at our disposal: prayer. I had trusted in my own ability, which got me nowhere.

I often wonder if things would have gotten so bad if I would have simply gone to God with my petitions first. I doubt it. This was a powerful lesson in my life, and one I have never forgotten. Immediately after I looked to God, He began to transform our lives.

It is often a first impulse to try and "fix" things ourselves. Sometimes we find ourselves in situations that seem so unfair—hard times that feel so unjust—wondering how we even got there! But God, in His infinite wisdom and profound mercy is there to help us through the tough times. He will be there in the darkest hour and will see you all the way through to days better than you could have ever imagined. All we have to do is reach out to Him and ask.

*O*KAY, GOD, IF YOU'RE LISTENING, WHY AREN'T YOU ANSWERING?

STAN TOLER

Faith is the substance of things hoped for, the evidence of things not seen.

HEBREWS 11:1

I had just closed my eyes for a brief afternoon nap. The conference in Dayton, Ohio, where I was speaking seemed to have drained all the energy out of me. That's when the phone rang, disturbing my sleep. The caller asked me to hurry to the Fayette County Hospital where my wife, Linda, had gone into labor. Moments after I arrived, Adam James Toler was born prematurely into the world, weighing a whopping eight pounds, ten ounces!

As I laid my head back down on the pillow just after midnight, I began to focus on the Sunday morning service I was to conduct the next day at Heritage Memorial Church. I was tired but anxious to tell the congregation about the birth of our second son.

At 4:00 A.M. the phone rang. It was the doctor.

"Come to the hospital quickly! Adam is having some difficulty," he said. I got dressed hurriedly and rushed to the hospital in record time!

As I arrived, I noticed that the infant care mobile unit from Children's Hospital was parked at the emergency entrance of the Fayette County Hospital. Nurses met me at the door to explain that they had performed emergency surgery, and it would be necessary to take Adam to the Columbus Children's Hospital. After meeting with Dr. Chang, we agreed that Adam needed a moment to bond with his mother before leaving the hospital. Because of an infection that Adam had developed and his difficulty breathing, the two had yet to experience a mother-son moment.

As the nurse lifted Adam from his isolette unit and presented him to his mother for the first time, hot tears poured from my eyes. Watching Linda hold Adam for that first moment and realizing that he might not live for another hour was overwhelming. Linda kissed Adam good-bye and watched intently as they rolled his isolette chamber from the room. As I hugged Linda, our tears mingled with the haunting thought that our son might not live.

"Linda," I said through tears, "who pastors the pastor? All these years of ministry, I have stood by and encouraged others. I've prayed prayers of comfort for many families, and here we are alone!"

Linda pulled me down close, and then she prayed a beautiful prayer of thanks for Adam, boldly asking God for a miracle.

The long drive to Children's Hospital in Columbus, Ohio, gave me time for thought and prayer. I pulled myself together, followed the medical team to the Infant Care Unit on the second floor, and braced myself for the worst.

To my surprise, there were more than thirty premature infants in that unit at Children's Hospital. Some of the babies weighed less than two pounds, and many were smaller than my hand. Adam, at eight pounds, ten ounces, looked like a "giant among mortals." But he was still a very sick baby, with a collapsed lung and a condition termed "serious."

Days and hours passed. To my surprise, my church family was gracious and caring. They watched over Linda in the Fayette County Hospital, and they made arrangements for my in-laws, James and Nadine Carter, to come to Ohio from south Georgia to watch over our four-year-old, Seth. They conducted daily prayer vigils at church and visited me regularly at the hospital. During all of their caregiving, I began to realize the importance of lay ministry. And I discovered that lay persons are the ones who can pastor the pastor!

While I was at Children's Hospital, I spent a lot of time with Adam. He was strapped down with tubes running everywhere, always flat on his back. He rarely moved or made a sound. My job at the hospital was to be near him and to constantly touch him. It was the nurses' view that a parent's touch was very important to the recovery of the child. I couldn't agree more. The healing from that contact was going both directions.

On the third day, after taking a short lunch break, I returned to the Infant Care Unit only to encounter nurses who explained that Adam had taken a turn for the worse.

"He might not live through the day," they said. Because they were performing emergency procedures, I was not allowed in the room. I rushed to a phone and began to call friends from California to Virginia, asking them to pray for Adam. Hundreds gathered at Heritage Memorial Church for prayer. Heaven was being bombarded for Adam James!

Two hours passed, and a nurse came to get me. A weak feeling went through my inner being. I was not optimistic. As I approached Adam, I noticed that he was face down on the bed, no diaper, his rear end sticking up in the air, and there was movement! I asked the nurse, "What does this mean?"

"Pastor," she explained, "it's the 'butt' sign."

"The butt sign?" I inquired.

"Yes, sir," she explained. "When we turn them over on their tummy, it means they are going to make it! Sir, your prayers have been answered. You have a healthy son, and he'll be going home soon!"

I was in a state of shock. "God has healed my son," I cried.

What rejoicing I felt that day! How ashamed I was of my own lack of faith, and yet how thrilled I was at the faith of my brothers and sisters in Christ. They had touched God for me.

$\mathcal{A}$ BRIGHT FUTURE

CLARENCE SMITH

The path of the righteous is like the first gleam of dawn, shining ever

brighter till the full light of day.

PROVERBS 4:18 NIV

"OPPORTUN-
ITY'S FAVORITE
DISGUISE IS
TROUBLE."

Frank Tyger

That was the last place I wanted to be—aboard an airplane headed to Connecticut for a VA rehabilitation program for the blind, hundreds of miles away from my home and family. I shifted in the seat and focused on the faint glow I knew must be the sunlight coming through the window, wondering what had happened to the eager 18-year-old kid I once was, on the way to U.S. Marine Corps boot camp back in 1960. The world was full of possibilities then; but those possibilities had become as dark and vague as my eyesight.

I had grown up in West Virginia hill country, one of twelve kids. No matter how tight money was, Mama made sure we never went hungry—she could fix a tasty meal with just a handful of vegetables and a sprinkle of spices. On chilly, gray days, all it took for me to feel warm again was a good whiff of whatever was bubbling in the cast-iron pot on the stove. She passed on her skills to us kids, and cooking became one of my favorite hobbies. The measuring and mixing of ingredients was a way of sorting out what was going on in my life.

Another constant in my childhood was faith. I could always count on someone, usually my aunt Callie May, taking me to our small, crowded church every Sunday. "Trust in the Lord and He'll always take care of you," she said. And I would stare at the flames in the potbellied coal stove that heated our church, daydreaming about the future God planned for me.

I thought I had found that future when I became a Marine. But in 1964, during a routine gas-mask training exercise, one of my lungs ruptured. I was rushed to surgery, but it was too late; doctors couldn't save the lung. For years, I battled one wicked bout of pneumonia after another. Finally, I was medically discharged from the service in 1969.

Coal was pretty much the only industry in my hometown, so—despite my missing lung—I went to work as an electrician in the mines. I married Helen in 1971, and soon we had our children, Tina and Jerry.

Sometimes it was hard facing the fact that I didn't have the physical energy to play ball with my son or give my daughter a piggyback ride, but I was proud that I was supporting them. Even when I had trouble breathing way down deep in the mines, I kept going because every day meant money toward a new cheerleading uniform for Tina or a fishing trip with Jerry.

In the mid '80s my remaining lung couldn't take it anymore, and I had to quit working. My family was forced to scrape by on my monthly disability pension from the VA. I fixed things around the house; I helped Helen in the kitchen. At least I was doing *something*.

Then in 1989 came a crushing blow: I had developed a brain tumor that left me unable to walk, talk, or eat. An operation restored most of my abilities, but I was partially paralyzed on my left side, deaf in one ear, and, worst of all, legally blind. The world was reduced to vague outlines weaving in and out of my vision like ghosts, taunting me with hints of what I would never again see. I had fought through pain and fatigue for years in the mines to have the means to make my children happy, and yet I could no longer even gaze at their smiles.

Day in and day out, I huddled in bed, shaking off my family's attempts to cheer me up, trying to sleep as much as possible so I didn't have to think about how useless I had become.

One afternoon I lay with my face buried in my pillow. *Why has this happened to me, Lord?* I asked. *I've always tried to do right by my family, my country, and by You. Why have You left me like this? I trust in You.*

"Come out with us," my wife coaxed gently. "It's a beautiful day."

"Don't feel like it," I mumbled.

Helen sat down on the bed beside me. "Jerry, listen, you can't go on like this. I really think you should go to that program the doctor told you about. That blind rehabilitation."

The thought of starting over again was just too overwhelming. I didn't even want to get out of bed. Why bother? I couldn't work; I couldn't find my way around the house; I couldn't even get myself a glass of water.

"What good will that do?" I said to Helen. "Three months trying to do all the things I can't do anymore."

"Is that any worse than lying here feeling the way you do now?" she said. "You've got to give this a try."

Eventually I didn't have the energy to argue with her anymore. So here I was, picking at bland airport food as my mind raced with fears—of getting sick on the plane, of not being met at the airport when I got to Connecticut, of what was in store for me at the program. I felt more afraid than I ever had.

A program instructor met me when I got off the plane, but I was still tense the whole drive to the blind center. *This will just make me feel more worthless,* I told myself. Instead of joining the others in the common area after the orientation that evening, I retreated to call my family.

"I can almost taste that chicken and mashed potatoes you're cooking from here, Honey," I said, clasping the receiver tightly with both hands. "Wish I was there." Helen gave me a pep talk, and after we hung up I groped my way to the window and opened it a crack to try to catch a scent of the vegetable garden they had taken us through. I thought of all the places I had been—in the Marines I had looked forward to each assignment as a new adventure, but now all I wanted was to go home. I shoved a hand in my pocket and ran a finger along the grooved metal of my house key. If only I could get back to the airport or even to a bus station, I could catch the first ride back. But I was trapped. *Okay, Lord, I'm here, now what?*

The next morning an instructor got me up, took me out into the center of town and began teaching me how to cross streets safely and get where I wanted to go. Next, she sent me out on my own. I had to be mighty resourceful to avoid getting stranded. By the end of the week I had begun to feel a little more confident. During group activities I got to know my classmates, some of whom were totally blind and in wheelchairs to boot. *If they can do this, maybe I can too,* I allowed.

Together we practiced basic things like buttoning our clothes correctly and cutting apples, then moved on to buying groceries and setting up systems to simplify finding items in cabinets. *Thank You, God, for my being able to walk out here in the fresh air,* I found myself thinking one day as I tapped down a sidewalk with a red-and-white cane.

One morning I awoke early with the urge to go outside. I made my way to the vegetable garden. I stood for a moment, inhaling the rich, earthy smell that reminded me of Mama's kitchen so long ago. Then I dropped to my knees. I dug my fingers into the soil and felt a turnip stem. A bee buzzed by my ear and the breeze sneaked under my shirt as I yanked the vegetable out of the earth. I brushed the dirt off that plump treasure, set it down and picked some tomatoes from vines nearby.

I breathed deeply. Peppermint. I crawled toward it and picked some, then caught another whiff of another spice—and another—rosemary, thyme, garlic, dill. Everywhere I turned I smelled yet another aroma from my childhood, and I rushed to touch and taste them all. Each time I harvested a spice, it was as if I were unearthing hope buried deep inside me—another possibility I had thought was lost. *Maybe there's still something out there for me,* I thought. I raised my head and felt the sun on my cheeks. *With Your help, Lord, I know I can find it.*

I fingered the smooth, waxy skin of sweet peppers and brushed crinkly lettuce leaves across my cheek. My stomach growled. *What a salad this would make!* I thought. For the first time since the brain tumor there was something I really wanted to do. I wanted to cook a mouthwatering meal just like Mama used to.

It took a little convincing, but the program directors let me and two friends make Thanksgiving dinner for the more than 40 other program participants. You name it, it was on the menu: roast turkey, dressing, ham, potato salad, green beans, macaroni salad, pineapple upside-down cake. And a salad with vegetables and spices from the garden. The feast went so well, I was offered a job in the kitchen. But I had a vision of my own.

"You know what?" I said to my new friends. "When I get back home, I'm going to open a restaurant. Folks in my neck of the woods are always saying they'd like a place where they can get a good, fast bite to eat."

"You kidding?" one guy said. "Look at all the work tonight took."

"I don't care. I've always loved to cook. And I know this'll go over big."

As I packed my belongings on the last day of the program, I checked for my keys and remembered how I had wished I had been able to get a plane or bus home that first night. Now I felt I could walk all the way home with what I had learned.

At the airport I greeted Helen and told her about my idea in the same breath. The next day, she drove us to the VA Regional Office.

My counselor led me into his office. "You're looking well, Jerry. How can I help you today?"

I poured out my restaurant idea, explaining that my wife would help me with the business side. "Sounds like you got yourself a plan there, Jerry," he said slowly. "We can help you with resources. But, you know," he added, "if you go through with this, you're going to lose your pension. And it's going to be a lot of hard work."

"Hard work never scared me any," I said. Helen and I put together a business plan. Two weeks later we got approval, and in October 1994 we opened The Roadside Sandwich and Pizza Shop. We make more than 100 items, and get most of our orders from locals and the coal companies.

"Did you really give up a government pension for all this work?" customers often ask me.

"Sure did," I always say. And I've never felt better about my life. I love to chop greens for my famous chef's salad as I listen to gospel music on the tape player and smell the bread baking. Maybe life's colors have faded, but its flavors are sharper than ever.

God had been taking care of me all along, leading me to a vision that was buried deep within me like the vegetables in the garden. He provided me with the ingredients and a dream for a better life, then left it up to me to make something out of them.

THE OLD MAN

RUBEN TIJERINA

My dear brothers...everyone should be quick to listen, slow to speak....

If anyone considers himself religious and yet does not keep a tight rein on

his tongue, he deceives himself and his religion is worthless.

JAMES 1:19,26 NIV

"IF YOU FEEL
DOG-TIRED
AT THE END
OF THE DAY,
IT MAY BE
BECAUSE YOU
GROWLED
ALL DAY."

Anonymous

*I*t was one of those days. Every traffic light turned red just as I approached, and every errand I had to run seemed to take longer than usual. Not to mention the meeting I had just gotten out of, in which my staff accountant had given me the numbers for that month. Things didn't look so good.

I had started a small company two years earlier, at what I had thought was God's direction, but now I was beginning to have my doubts. Had I been wrong to leave my steady income at the engineering firm where I had worked for fifteen years?

Stressed to the max, I had taken the afternoon off and hoped to clear my mind with a round of golf. It looked like I had just enough time to get in eighteen holes before I needed to meet some colleagues for dinner. I called up a friend who agreed to meet me at the country club within the hour.

When I arrived, my friend was not yet there. As I retrieved my clubs and checked in at the desk, my cell phone rang. My friend was running a bit late and wanted me to start without him.

"Will nothing go right today?" I grumbled to myself as I gathered my things and headed to the course.

Apparently nothing would. I got in line for the first hole, and my thoughts strayed back to the company. *What were we going to do?* I fretted and fumed behind an elderly gentleman and his wife who were just preparing for the first hole. I smiled cordially at them as I waited, but my patience had just about reached its limit.

The old man seemed to take forever to choose his club, much less to tee off. As he hit his ball with a shaky swing, and it veered significantly off course, I suppressed a groan of irritation. *What is this guy doing playing golf here?* I thought to myself. *He's awful. He can't even hit the ball with a straight swing!*

Eventually, the older couple moved on to the second hole, and I was able to tee off. My shot was beautiful, arcing perfectly through the air and landing on the green. *Now that's the way it should be done!* I thought as I headed down the course. One more perfect shot, and I was two under par. *Maybe I should give the old guy some lessons.* I snorted under my breath at the thought.

As I reached the tee-off point for the second hole, the elderly man was struggling to pull a club out of his golf bag. His wife reached over to try and help him, and as they fumbled around, I felt my irritation begin to rise again. *I wonder if it would be rude if I asked them if I could tee off first,* I thought, but just then I turned to see my friend arriving. He waved hello from a distance and then hurried to join me. He caught up with me just as it was finally my turn to tee off on the second hole.

"I could have been done by now," I exclaimed in exasperation, "if it weren't for that old geezer in front of us!"

"Oh! Do you mean Mr. Davidson?" My friend squinted his eyes and peered ahead of us on the course. "I thought that was him! I'm so glad to see him out on the course today."

I stopped mid-swing and turned to face my friend. "What are you talking about?"

"Mr. Davidson. That man in front of you. He suffered a stroke six months ago. He was partially paralyzed on one side, and has been in physical therapy for months. He used to be a professional golfer, but since the stroke, he has been so self-conscious about his handicap that he hasn't even touched a golf club. Mrs. Davidson has been after him to get him out here—

looks like she finally did. Good for him!"

I felt about two feet tall. I had been so uptight about the little inconveniences of life that I had forgotten to take on an attitude of gratitude. While I was impatiently tapping my foot to be able to finish my golf game on time, the man just in front of me was facing one of the greatest challenges of his life.

I repented on the spot. And after we had all finished the course, I shook Mr. Davidson's shaky hand.

"Good game," was all I had to say. He beamed. "Son, I overheard you on your cell phone earlier. Am I to understand you have just started your own company?"

I nodded, and he went on. "Well, I have been looking for a small company in which to invest some money. When would be a convenient time for us to meet and talk about it?"

My friend and I looked at each other, and I stammered in disbelief, "Why don't you give me a call tomorrow?"

The old man I had originally scorned ultimately saved my company. And I learned an even more valuable lesson about life in the process; a lesson that built an anchor of strong personal character in my life.

$\mathcal{K}$EEP YOUR EYE ON THE BALL

MICHAEL DIRMEIER

Rejoice in the Lord always. I will say it again: Rejoice!

PHILIPPIANS 4:4 NIV

Baseball may be America's favorite pastime, but it sure wasn't mine. When I was a kid, I would volunteer for the outfield, and then stand as far back as I could, praying that the ball would not come my way. Once, when I swung and missed at an easy pitch, my gym teacher rolled the ball toward me on the ground and asked if I wanted to play golf.

Now that I'm grown, I've learned to appreciate the game, even to the point of becoming a Texas Rangers fan. I have never played as an adult, but I wanting to give Christopher, my eight-year-old son, the chance to try. I signed him up on a Little League team.

At Christopher's first game, I nervously watched as he

stepped up to bat. *God, please help him be different at this game than I was.* "Come on, son," I called out, hoping he could hear my encouragement. "Keep your eye on the ball!"

The pitch came, Christopher swung...and missed. Another pitch, another miss. This kept up until my son was finally declared, "You're out!"

Christopher's bat did not connect with the ball for the entire game. I braced myself after the game to comfort a frustrated and upset little boy, but instead I was greeted with smiles.

"Daddy, did you see me out there?"

"Yes, son, I sure did."

"Oooo, look, hot dogs! Can I have one?"

The crushing defeat seemed to have been forgotten in the excitement of a hot dog stand. "Sure," I replied, as he chattered his order to the vendor. *He's taking this so well,* I thought. *But we'll get some practice sessions in, and he'll do better in the next game. There was a whole season ahead of us, after all.*

But it was not to be. Christopher was the proverbial "chip off the old block." Week after week, game after game, strikeout after strikeout.

"Good try," became my mantra. Several times he came so close to connecting with the ball—but that was it: close, but still a strike.

"Thanks, Dad!" Christopher would say cheerfully, a big

smile spreading over his face at my encouragement.

I began to pace the sidelines each time he was up to bat. Each missed swing, I began to feel was my missed swing. Each strikeout, as Christopher returned to the dugout to laugh with his friends, I worried, *Are they laughing at him?* I kept expecting him to give up in defeat, but instead he looked like he was having fun.

One spring afternoon, after Christopher struck out as usual, he came over to ask me and my wife for some money for the soda machine.

"Great job out there, kiddo!" my wife exclaimed.

"You were pretty close on a couple of those swings, son. Just try to keep your eye on the ball next time." I felt the need to give helpful instruction, but Chris just shrugged it off.

"Okay, Dad!" He flashed a smile and then ran back to the dugout, high-fiving his friends as he put his helmet back on his head. I shook my head in disbelief. How could he still be so cheerful after an entire season of never hitting the ball?

"Lighten up," my wife seemed to have read my thoughts. "If Christopher isn't worried about hitting the ball, you shouldn't be either. He's just a kid, and he's having fun. That is the point, in case you've forgotten."

How can he be having fun? I wondered as I watched Christopher step up to bat yet again. Every time I struck out when I played, I could barely look my teammates in the eye. Every time I missed catching that easy fly ball, my face burned in shame. After every game, I wanted to crawl in a hole. *This must be hard on him too,* I thought. *He still needs my encouragement.*

Strike one.

Strike two.

"Come on, son! You can do it!" I called out encouragement.

I'd like to say that at that point, Christopher swung the bat and hit a home run, but that wasn't the case. He struck out yet again. I closed my eyes and hung my head in defeat. But when I glanced back up, Christopher was trotting over to the soda machine.

A minute later, he was sharing a grape soda with his mom and me. After a big swig, he smiled at me like he'd just hit the game-winning home run, purple lining his mouth. "Did you see me out there, Dad?"

As he ran back out to the field, he turned and gave me a thumbs-up. A thumbs-up! He truly was having fun! And all at once I realized that I had a decision to make. I could continue in my present attitude of frustration and defeat, or I could join in my son's attitude of fun and good sportsmanship. As I watched Christopher out on the field, it dawned on me that my prayer had been answered. The game of baseball was different for him than it was for me. No matter how well he did or whether or not his team won the game, he had found a way to have fun. And, yes, that was the point.

I grinned back at him and returned his thumbs-up. Later, after the game, we headed over to the hot dog vendor. As he happily chattered off his order, I patted his back. "Hey, Sport, I am so proud of you," I told him. "I like the way you play the game."

Our relationship changed that very day. My son grew up to be a champion all right, a champion youth counselor. He now works with troubled boys who have no father of their own. I'd like to think I had a hand in who he became, especially through the choice I made that day at the baseball field to let him play the game his way instead of mine.

ARMS WIDE OPEN

EMILIO CASTILLO

(As told to Mick Thurber)

Bear with each other and forgive whatever grievances you may have against

one another. Forgive as the Lord forgave you.

COLOSSIANS 3:13 NIV

I sat for hours in a dimly lit cell that night remembering my days as a migrant farm worker in the small Midwestern town where I'd come to live. Those days were often spent working long hours. But they were good days. Now suddenly my life had dramatically changed.

During the last ten years I had become affiliated with the local "Mexican Mafia." This gang was the scourge of the city and I was its most prolific drug dealer. If there had been a serious crime committed, I was the prime suspect.

I lived in the fast lane. I had it all—new cars, new trucks, new house, and pockets full of money. I kept reminding myself of that as I sat in the county jail. Just twenty-four hours earlier, I had it all. Now it was all gone.

I had been caught selling drugs, framed by my best friend and partner in crime, Lonnie. For years we terrorized the community, pushing drugs and committing burglaries, but now he turned me in to the police in an attempt to protect himself from being arrested. Because of him I was going to federal prison for six years. I made a vow that I would not rest until he paid for his betrayal. My hatred for him grew so intense that all I could think about was cutting him into pieces.

A year of pain and hurt passed slowly in my prison cell, one day at a time. Things grew worse. My oldest son despised me. My wife was under incredible pressure as she tried to provide for our four children by herself. All I could do was sit in prison and hate my life and Lonnie more and more each day.

Deperately searching for answers, I went to a prison church service. I was consumed with fear and felt so helpless as I sat in that service. As I listened to this simple preacher-boy who spoke of peace, forgiveness, and a new start, my heart welled up within me. In front of the other three hundred inmates in attendance that day, I suddenly stood up. In a loud voice I asked the preacher, "Can you show me how to receive Jesus into my life?"

The preacher opened his Bible and read Romans 10:9:

"That if you confess with your mouth that Jesus is Lord and believe in your heart that God has raised Him from the dead, you shall be saved." Suddenly, it was as if Jesus stood in that prison service with His arms opened wide. He was willing to take me in, regardless of my past, regardless of the fact that I was in prison.

I was forever changed. That night Jesus Christ became the center of my life. All the pain, all the fear, all the hate was gone. God made me a new man in Christ. Though each day, for the next five years, I woke up to see bars and guards surrounding me, I was no longer a prisoner. I was free in Christ. I believed what God said in Acts 16:31: "Believe on the Lord Jesus Christ, and you will be saved, you and your household."

The day I walked out of prison, I went home and never looked back. God fulfilled His promise to me by restoring my family.

God put it in my heart to find the pastor who had reached out to me in my youth, over thirty years ago. I found his name in the yellow pages. Just two weeks after being in this pastor's church, God spoke to him about me. The pastor told me that God wanted me to start a ministry in the same town where I lived before I went to prison. I couldn't believe it. I was already making plans to sell everything I had and get as far away from this place as I could. In this small community, I had been nothing but a disgrace and an embarrassment to my family.

God began to encourage me through His Word. With the love and support from a local church, I obeyed God and began to spread the good news of Jesus in the very town where I had been arrested.

After about three years, God told me to carry my ministry over to another nearby city. He told me, "I have gone ahead of you and prepared the way for you. I will place people along the path that will help you." Little did I know that God would bring along an old companion of mine. God had a reunion planned for two former friends.

He was the last person I ever expected to see. I had just finished preaching a Sunday morning sermon when he stepped through the back doorway of our small mission church. I walked toward the man and stood face-to-face with Lonnie, the very person who had helped send me to prison. I was overcome with the realization that God's love and forgiveness were bigger than both of us. As I looked into Lonnie's eyes, my years of hatred for him melted away. With my arms opened wide, we embraced and I forgave Lonnie as God had forgiven me.

He told me of his journey over the last seven years. He, too, was sent to prison not long after I was sentenced. And he, too, met the Savior behind the bars that held him.

In a moment God brought us back together and now He has sent us out together. Once again as a team, but now Lonnie and I serve our Lord, delivering the message of God's forgiveness and salvation to one of our city's worst areas for drugs and violence.

It is with great fulfillment that we share, with anyone who will listen about this God Who stands with His arms opened wide.

*W*AIT FOR ME, DADDY!

BYARD HILL

Listen to your father, who gave you life,

and do not despise your mother when she is old.

PROVERBS 23:22 NIV

"IT IS MUCH
EASIER TO
BECOME A
FATHER THAN
TO BE ONE."

Kent Nerburn

"Wait for me, Daddy!"

I was used to having to hurry to keep up with Daddy's long-legged stride, but I still wanted to follow him everywhere he went.

It was a not-very-well-kept secret that for most of his life, Daddy had wanted a son, but instead, he was forced to put up with me, his only child, a daughter. I tried hard to do the things that a son would do, but I was clearly meant to be a girl—not even a tomboy sort of girl, but the girliest of girls, with frilly dresses and tea parties to boot.

But when Dad went out to harvest the fields atop his enormous John Deere tractor, I still wanted to be with him. I ran out behind him, "Wait for me, Daddy!"

"Okay, Pumpkin, hop on up," he chuckled as he watched me try to climb aboard. Then his big, strong arms lifted me up to sit securely in front of him as he maneuvered the tractor through the fields.

Daddy wasn't chuckling so loudly the day he tried to take me fishing. "Wait for me, Daddy!" I called out as he set off down the path to the river, rod and reel in hand.

Fishing sure was boring, I soon found out, that is, until Daddy reeled in a big one! It lay, wet and slippery and gasping for breath on the riverbank. Daddy cut it loose and then placed it into a half-submerged basket. A little later, as he wandered farther down the river, I decided the fish needed a name. The fish was christened "Max" and soon it seemed to me that Max didn't really like captivity. I furtively glanced toward Daddy, who was concentrating so hard on catching another fish that he wasn't watching me. One flick of my finger on the latch to the basket, and Max was free once again.

Daddy was none too happy with my values of freedom for all of God's creatures, and the next time we went fishing I got to bring along my baby dolls and puzzle books. *If I had been a boy, Daddy would like fishing with me so much better,* the nagging thought came, and just wouldn't leave.

But I still wanted to be a part of Daddy's life. "Wait for

me, Daddy!" I called out as often as I could. Daddy hiked mountains with me trailing behind; we rode bikes, went camping, and even changed a flat tire on the car.

Eventually I grew older, and my interests turned to more "girly" things, but Daddy still waited for me. He taught me how to drive, and even though I had become more interested in shopping at the mall and learning how to apply mascara than practicing football in the backyard, he still was my daddy.

Some years later, Daddy drove me off to college, and I'll never forget as he drove away slowly, waving his hand out the window. Was that a tear in Daddy's eye? *Wait for me, Daddy,* I thought to myself. *I'll be home soon.*

That first semester I was invited to a meeting held at a church not too far from the university. I went along, and was surprised to hear a man talking about his relationship with God—and it wasn't boring! That night I gave my heart to my Heavenly Father, but instead of distancing me from my earthly father, this new relationship with God only made my daddy more dear to me.

As Christmas approached that year, I found myself wishing my dad had a real and exciting relationship with God like the one I had discovered. When I noticed a small, brown Bible on a sale rack in the mall, I thought, *Maybe I should buy this for Daddy for Christmas.* But just as quickly, I dismissed the thought. *That's too girly of a present. Daddy wouldn't want that.* I figured he'd prefer a fishing rod or some new tools for his toolbox, but something in me persisted.

When Daddy opened the Bible on Christmas day, I realized my fears about his gift were unfounded. He acted just like he always did. "Thanks, Pumpkin," he said as he kissed my forehead.

But as time went on, I began to wonder. *Would Daddy ever actually read the Bible I had given him? Would he ever find the relationship with God that I had experienced?*

The semester went on, and my life continued, busy as usual, full of new people, classes, homework, and exams. But one day shortly before spring finals were to begin, my mother called. "Daddy's sick," was all she needed to say.

The sight of my big, strong daddy in a hospital bed was startling. The cancer had been slowly taking over. The doctors were going to try to save him through surgery, but it didn't look good.

"It's okay, Pumpkin," Daddy said as I laid my head on his chest and wept.

As they wheeled Daddy into surgery, I noticed something that looked familiar to me. A small, brown Bible lay on his bedside table. *Had Daddy been reading the Bible I had gotten him for Christmas?* My hands trembled as I picked it up and then turned to my mother with a questioning look. She smiled as she told me that Daddy had read my Bible—that he had found God in the last few months, and that he knew that if he died, he would go to Heaven.

Daddy didn't make it through the surgery. We buried him on a sunny day in late spring, but as I stood at his grave stone, I knew that I would see him again.

"Wait for me, Daddy," I whispered. "I'll see you soon."

*W*HISTLIN' WILLIE

PAT MIDDLETON

Two are better than one....If one falls down, his friend can help him up.

But pity the man who falls and has no one to help him up!

ECCLESIASTES 4:9,10

Could I ever explain how lost and alone I felt sitting at the desk in his den, his books and papers scattered around me, his photographs up on the wall? My father had just died. And I found myself in that old chair of his, half expecting him to come into the room at any moment and catch me there. If only he could talk me through my grief and help me find my way.

Above me hung models of every plane he ever flew, suspended from the ceiling on thin black thread. And there he was, up on the wall in all his glory—his life shown in the pictures that were carefully displayed on a backdrop of dark paneling. My father as a young man in his leather flight jacket, a silver plane behind him. That wonderful, boyish smile of his was repeated in almost every snapshot, from his World War II days to his days at Cape Kennedy. Looking at my father's smile, seeing him young and strong again, I still couldn't bring myself to believe that this man, Stan Middleton, was gone.

He had been a pilot in World War II, splitting his time between tours of combat in Europe and stints stateside, where he helped develop techniques to fly B-17 bombers north to Alaska without having them ice up. After the war, he worked on jet engines for General Electric, and then got a job at NASA to help with the Apollo launches. Sitting at his desk, I felt incredibly proud of my father.

I had a great wife and family. In addition, I had a wonderful career as a counselor, which gave me great satisfaction. But it seemed I had never accomplished anything like he had. The war, the space program—he'd been a leader in a heroic generation of Americans.

I leafed through his clippings and papers, absently fingering the wooden arm of his chair, trying to piece together the things he told me those last couple of days. He had gone so quickly, less than a week. I had been at his bedside, rubbing his cold hands, as dad slipped in and out of consciousness. We shared long spells of silence, but he also shared things about his life, things that he'd never told me before. He was surprised by how fast the years had gone by. "Almost eighty years, Pat, and it's gone just like that," he said.

He lay there listless much of the time, then he'd turn onto his side, fully awake, asking to have more ice or water. He'd cough and take a sip and appear like a man who would live another 20 years. The next moment, he looked like a man who'd just taken his final breath. At one point, in the small hours of the night, my father suddenly sat up on his elbows. He wanted to tell me a story, he said, the story of Whistlin' Willie. So I propped him up with some pillows and he talked while I listened.

In the war, he'd made long bombing runs over Germany. More than once in the night, the pilots had flown back to England only to find their airfield outside London fogged in. With wounded airmen onboard and dangerously low on fuel, the formation would limp on to the next base. Some of the damaged planes never made it. It seemed an extravagant waste, the planes and men surviving bombing runs only to be lost to the English fog.

This didn't sit well with Captain Middleton. In his spare time, he and a flight engineer worked on a battle-damaged B-17. It kept them busy during the long days when they didn't fly, rebuilding the ram-shackle aircraft, part by part, piece by piece.

One part they couldn't replace was the propeller on one of the engines. The prop had been hit with a .50-caliber shell. It made an incredible wail as wind streamed through the hole when the engines cranked up. "It was absolutely piercing," Dad said, "just about the loudest thing I'd ever heard. But it could still fly." Hearing the plane taxi down the runway one day, someone in the control tower dubbed it "Whistlin' Willie." The name stuck.

Whistlin' Willie would never be combat-ready, but my dad convinced the control tower to let him test fly it over the base. It must have been then—circling the base on that ribbon of sound—that the idea came to him. Could he lead those other planes through the fog with this one?

My father went to the navigation specialists: Was there a way to rig up some device on the old plane to locate the runway through the fog? He went to the radio technicians: Could he fix on a radio signal and use a locator, compass, clock and altimeter to plot a flight path? Only after he had everything lined up did my father approach the commanding officer for the go-ahead.

The morning was foggy when word arrived that a squadron of planes was returning to base. They'd sustained heavy fire and there were wounded men. The C.O. volunteered to hold a radio microphone button down for a constant signal. Radar was in its infancy and this was how Dad might find the base through the worst weather conditions. The call was sent out

to the approaching fliers: "Look for Whistlin' Willie," the
base radioman told them. "He's gonna lead you home through
the fog."

Not knowing what this meant, the pilots searched the sky.
They were ragged, tired, and afraid of the fog, thick as soup
below them. But Captain Middleton put on his flight suit and
throttled that old B-17 screaming down the runway. The old
barn of a plane took flight, circling over the signal of the radio
microphone, the windshield streaked and wet with the clouds
Dad was flying through. The sound of the engines and
propellers thundered so loud he could feel them in his chest as
he turned and turned, constantly checking the clock, the signal
locator and altimeter in the widening circle over the airbase.

The first glimpse of sun broke across his wings as he
breached the surface of clouds. Then he was circling over a
floor of gray cotton, London hidden from view, the B-17 rattling
as if ready to fall apart at the seams. And there, in the distance,
he caught the glint of light from the other planes approaching.

The returning planes fell into formation behind him, those
that were either damaged or carrying wounded moving into line
first. He could take only a few planes at a time, so he led the
first string down through the fog, the pilots all trusting the lead
of Captain Middleton and Whistlin' Willie.

The pilots had to depend on one another to provide visual

confirmation that they were taking the right flight path through the fog, the followers becoming leaders for those behind them. And if a pilot got spooked by the fog and couldn't see, the control tower told him to lean out the window and listen carefully for the screaming propeller up ahead; the sound would help guide him safely to the airstrip.

Dad led the way until the airfield could be seen. Fifty yards from the tarmac, he pulled up and buzzed the control tower. Then he banked the plane back into the fog, circling up for the next set of planes.

"I can't tell you how many planes we guided down through the fog in those last months of the war," my father said, "but it was the best thing I've ever done in my life." He fell silent and closed his eyes after that, his cheeks more hollow than I remembered, his breaths shallow and growing quiet as he fell asleep. It was the last story my father told me. After that it was mostly ice chips, cool washcloths, and squeezes of his hand until he passed early in the morning.

After his death, the image of that plane holding a string of souls by a thread of sound—its whistle in the dark—kept coming back to me. I wondered what my father meant by this story. But I had to deal with mundane matters like his will, his insurance policy, his bank accounts. Besides, there was the raw grief.

Now, as I sat quiet at his desk, though, staring at the photos on the wall, my father seemed to smile down at me with that same boyish grin of his, it seemed I could hear him say, *You may be lost in a fog of grief now, but you'll make it through. You'll find your way home.*

How? I wondered staring at the photos and remembering that last war story.

The answer came suddenly to my heart. *Follow the lead of others. There will be people to help you—your minister, lawyer, counselor, friends, wife, children. When you can't see the way, God will give you the people to guide you. Listen for them. That is how God will show you His way.*

At last the fog was clearing.

*W*HEN I WAS A PRODIGAL SON

DON HALL

(as told to Nanette Thorsen-Snipes)

As far as the east is from the west,

So far has He removed our transgressions from us.

PSALM 103:12, KJV

At the age of seventeen, I found myself sitting in a jail cell wondering how things could have gone so wrong in my life. I didn't know it then, but looking back, I felt a lot like the prodigal son of the Bible.

It was two days after Thanksgiving. Clouds were slung low across the sky and overshadowing with rain that cold day in 1983. My mom, my stepdad, Jim, and my younger brother and sister had gone to the grocery store. Before they got home, the phone rang, and I answered it.

After asking for my mother, the person on the phone said,

"Tell her that Benny hung himself." It felt as though someone struck me in the gut. Benny was my dad.

"Is he dead?" I asked, holding my breath and hoping it wasn't true. I couldn't even cry. But the pain left an empty hole in me because I didn't really know my dad. When the answer came back, "Yes," I sat down to absorb what had happened.

A flood of memories came back. It seemed like a re-run of one of those unbelievable, yet true, stories. My mother had faced my dad's rage one weekend—at the end of a gun. She finally talked him into putting it down. After he went to work, she packed our bags and we moved out. My brother was seven and I was four, yet I vividly remember being in the motel room where we hid out for a week. I had on my cowboy outfit that day, and Mom was crying.

Maybe that's one reason why I stayed angry all those years. I was angry at my father for trying to hurt Mom. Later, I was angry because he died before I could get to know him.

Nothing ever went right for me after my dad died. I couldn't concentrate or learn. I finally quit school in the tenth grade. I went to work as a roofer, a carpet cleaner, anything I could do to earn money.

My anger continued to grow. I often made life miserable for everyone around me by drinking. Alcohol brought on more anger, which made me lose my temper. It was nothing for me to put my fist through a wall or kick in a door. I was arrested several times for driving under the influence of alcohol.

One day, I became angry because the bike I'd bought wasn't working right. I picked the ten-speed bicycle up over my head and began screaming obscenities. I slammed it repeatedly into the ground until it lay in a crumpled heap.

Mom and Jim became alarmed at my uncontrollable rage and took me to see a counselor. I had nothing to say to a shrink. I just sat there and waited for him to quit talking. After the third session, he gave up and told Mom he couldn't help me if I wouldn't communicate, which suited me just fine.

My drinking worsened, and I had bouts with depression, staying in bed for days. I also started hanging out with bad company, and earned myself some dangerous enemies.

One day a bullet hit my car as I drove down the highway. When someone kicked down the basement door, which led to my bedroom, I too became alarmed. I guess that's why I took the gun from my parents' closet. I never kept it loaded, but its presence made me feel safe.

The next evening I drove to the hotel where my brother worked. After parking my car, I went straight toward the bar.

Inside, a strong, burly man said, "Son, I need to see your ID." Because I didn't have one, I tried to muscle my way past the guy. He became angry and shoved me. I shoved back. The next thing I knew he smacked me in the jaw, and I hit the floor. I jumped up, waving the gun in his face.

Meanwhile someone had called the police and in a split second I heard them say, "Freeze!" I turned to my left where three policemen stood in a firing stance, their guns drawn and aimed directly at me. To my right, I looked down the barrel of another officer's gun. The scene was chaotic. The police shouted, "Drop your weapon! Get your hands up on the wall!" I was then handcuffed and taken to jail.

So, for the fourth or fifth time, I sat in the county jail with the stench of bodily fluids and sweaty men surrounding me. I didn't worry. Whenever I was caught driving under the influence of alcohol, my parents always posted bail for me. So I was shocked when I called for them to get me out and Mom said, "No."

I didn't realize at the time that they had been praying for me. They had decided to let go and entrust me to God. But all I could see were the bars on that jail cell and no way out. I paced the floor like a wild animal. After a while, I knew I was in real trouble, and so I said a simple prayer: *God, please help me. All I want is a decent life.*

A few days later, a friend and his father posted bail for me. Angrily, I went home and packed my things, never once speaking to my parents. Then I moved in with my friend.

Within a year, I met a beautiful young woman. We later married and now have two wonderful children. Several months later, my wife and I both turned our lives over to God. In fact, I began spending many of my evenings sharing my story with men in state prisons. I told them about God and his miraculous transformation on my life.

I still regret all the pain I caused my parents. One recent Christmas, while my wife and the kids were at Mom's, my stepdad and I went to the grocery store. While in the cab of the truck with music softly playing in the background, I said, "Jim, can you ever forgive me for all the pain I've put you through?"

The man I knew as my dad looked at me and smiled. "I've already forgiven you, Donnie," he said. Then he put his arm around me. I couldn't help thinking of the prodigal son and how our Heavenly Father always welcomes us home, too.

*D*AD WOULDN'T SAY

JOHN ASHCROFT

Love is patient, love is kind. It does not envy, it does not boast,

it is not proud. It is not rude, it is not self-seeking,

it is not easily angered, it keeps no record of wrongs.

1 CORINTHIANS 13:4-5, NIV

As part of a long ministerial career, my father served as the president of a small, liberal arts college in the Midwest. After more than fifteen years, it became apparent that his vision for the future of the college differed somewhat from that of the board of trustees. I was never aware of any actual points of contention, but once my father realized that these differences were unlikely to be resolved, he tendered his letter of resignation to the trustees.

This occurred in early fall. The board sat on this letter until late spring. Then, just days before commencement exercises in May, the board formally accepted his resignation.

If the board had waited a few dozen hours, a handful of

days, my father could have handed out the diplomas and congratulated the graduating seniors he had known and loved as president of the college. As it was, the abrupt timing of his termination could easily have been construed as malicious.

Many students and not a few faculty were extremely upset. The students expected to get their diplomas from my father. After all, he had been their president for three years, eight months, and all but a few days of their academic careers!

Yet when my father called to tell me the news, he was remarkably dispassionate. It was all very matter-of-fact. "John, I thought you should know that I'm leaving the college. I submitted my resignation last autumn, and the board has chosen to act on it."

Remarkably, my father would not allow a single negative to enter our conversation. Though I tried to probe him and find out what had really happened, it was clear to me that he held no grudges. In fact, the posture he took astonished me. Instead of feeling bitter, my father had a profound sense of gratitude for the work he had enjoyed while serving as president of a college.

The controversy was aggravated because the board of trustees named a replacement within days. Normally it takes a good year or more to hire a new college president. This led some to wonder if my father had simply been held on until the board found a new president, and then, once the choice was made, he was let go instantly.

Dad was not blind to all this; he had been a college president for almost two decades, and though many suggested he had every reason to be upset, my father never reflected any of that. Neither did he ever complain. On the contrary, he continued to befriend and serve all of the individuals involved in the awkward decision to replace him days before the school term ended.

My father was fairly well known, with good standing, and more than a few people looked up to him. They watched to see how he would react. If he had decided to seek vengeance or spread negative gossip, he would have found many willing ears. Instead, my father went out of his way to endorse every aspect of the college and even the individuals involved in terminating his service.

What my father didn't say about this situation told me as much about him as what he did say on many other occasions. I learned that he was a man who didn't nurse, feed, or build grudges. He didn't ask his family to bear the emotional strain and stress of his responsibilities while he served as president, and he wasn't about to change course, asking us to bear the strain of an indecorous dismissal.

He seemed incapable of holding a grudge—a lesson that has served me well in public office.

*T*HE EVERYDAY, STREET-WALKIN', DOOR-BANGIN' SALESMAN

As a man thinketh in his heart, so is he.

PROVERBS 23:7

*I*n 1970 I returned from my tour of duty in Vietnam with big plans about what I was going to accomplish. It wouldn't be easy. I had no real work experience, no skills, and no education to speak of. I knew one thing, though—God had seen me safely through the war, and He'd be sure to take care of me, back home.

The only job I could find in Lick Creek, Illinois, was in a quarry, drilling rocks all day for $2.75 an hour. My wife, Vickie, and I lived in a rented three-room shack. We had no water on the property, and only one room had electricity, thanks to an extension cord hooked up to a nearby farmhouse.

But we had our dreams, and that was enough.

We didn't get many visitors, so I stepped outside one day when I heard a car coming down our dirt driveway. A shiny new Cadillac Fleetwood glided to a stop in front of the shack. A tall, thin man got out of the car, threw a cigarette butt into the flower patch, and smiled. "I've got a marvelous product to show you," he said, "something you really need." He went around to the trunk and pulled out a big box, opening it to show me a shiny set of pots and pans. "This here is top-of-the-line West Bend Waterless Cookware," he said. "Nothin' like it."

They were nice, and we needed pans. But what I really liked was the man's Cadillac Fleetwood. A lot nicer than my rusty old Pontiac. *If this guy can own a boat like that, I bet I could too,* I thought. Vickie and I filled out the paperwork for the pans, then fished a wad of bills out of the sugar bowl, just enough to cover the $38.95 down payment. "Hey," I said, handing him the money, "I'd like a job selling those pans."

"Can't help you there," he said. "Enjoy the cookware. It'll be on its way." He slammed the Caddy's door and drove away.

But I just couldn't get the thought of selling those pans out of my mind. Looking up the man's number, I called him at home to inquire again about a job. No dice. I kept on phoning, and by the twelfth call—and probably just to get me off his back—he said he'd give me a shot. "But it'll cost you three hundred dollars up front for a sample set," he said. *Three hundred dollars? That's more than two weeks' pay.* I talked it over with Vickie that night and we prayed about it until I felt sure about things. The next day, I pawned my guitar and our camera, the only possessions we owned that were of any value.

The salesman seemed surprised to see me, and even more surprised to see my money. Can of soda in hand, he led me to the garage, where there was a set of cookware that had been repossessed. He wrapped the pots and pans in newspaper and stuffed them into an old suitcase, along with some wrinkled order forms. Then he handed me the suitcase and said, "Come back next week and I'll train you."

"Wait a minute—" I started to say, but he'd already shut the door in my face. *I can't wait that long!* I worried as I drove away. I had only ten days to redeem my guitar and camera from the pawn shop. *I have to make some money fast!*

I drove into town, parked the car, and started knocking on doors. I had no idea what I was going to say, but I just knew I was going to sell some pots and pans. So I said the first thing that popped into my head: "Hello! I might look like your everyday, street-walkin', door-bangin' salesman, but I've got the neatest set of pots and pans you ever did see. Could I come in and show 'em to you, please?"

I sold eleven sets that first week and headed for the pawn shop.

I was red hot. When I went back to see the salesman, he looked stunned. "Training?" he said. "Looks like I don't have to teach you anything. You just go on and keep doing what you've been doing."

I quit my job at the quarry and started selling full-time. There were good days and bad days, yet never quite as much luck as I'd had that first week. But I managed to put away some money. By my second year, my wife and I had saved enough to buy a trailer home. The place had electricity and I dug a well out back and ran a pipe so we finally had indoor plumbing.

Soon after, we found out Vickie was pregnant. With no insurance, it would be hard covering all the new expenses, but we were excited with our new journey and certain God would see us through.

The day Vickie gave birth to our twin boys was one of the happiest day of my life. But all that joy was quickly shattered by the news from the doctor telling us that our sons had been born with a serious lung disorder. Within two weeks they were dead. The hardest thing I ever had to do was go to that funeral for my sons.

The second hardest was forcing myself to go back to work. I never knew I could feel so low. Vickie seemed to think that going back to work would help me. And we needed the money desperately. I drove into town, parked my car, hauled my sample case out of the trunk. Lugging it door to door, I launched into my pitch: "I might look like your everyday, street-walkin'…" I couldn't get people to even look at my cookware, let alone buy any of it. At the end of the day I went home feeling like a flop. And I ached with grief.

When I'd first begun selling, I was driven by the desire to get my guitar and camera back from the pawn shop, then to get the trailer. I enjoyed building a new life for Vickie and the family we had planned. Sure, it would've been tough coming up with money for clothes, shoes, toys and the other things babies need, but I welcomed those expenses. Now all I was left with were substantial bills for doctors and the funeral home. All the work I'd been doing seemed hollow, meaningless.

I couldn't stand being broke again, but I was too proud to borrow or take a handout. One night I told Vickie, "If I don't make a sale tomorrow, I'm going to go to the quarry and see if I can get my old job back." Really, it was the only thing I knew to do. Vickie was still struggling with her own grief, and honestly, I wasn't sure how we were going to get through this. I was so down I couldn't even pray much about it.

Like me, the Pontiac was running on fumes and I couldn't afford to fill the tank. So that night I got on my bike and pedaled around, picking up empty pop bottles to return for the deposit money. I collected enough for two gallon's worth of gas. When I went to the gas station with a can, the attendant asked, "Hey, how's it going with those pots and pans, Dave?"

"Oh, it's going great!" I couldn't bear to admit how bad things were. Not to anyone. Later at home as I held Vickie, she murmured something to me. "As terrible as losing the boys feels, David, I get a little better day by day. The Lord is helping me, I know."

The next morning as I drove into town, I parked the car and started going from door to door. It was a hot summer day, and my sample case felt heavy in my hand, as if it were filled with all the troubles of the past few months. I couldn't provide for my wife, I couldn't save my sons, and now I couldn't even close one lousy deal. *Lord,* I cried silently, *You have to help me, too.*

I was heading down Cherry Street toward my car, already planning what I'd say to the foreman at the quarry the next day. Then I noticed a man on a ladder painting the eaves of his house. Something prodded me: *Give it one last shot.*

I went to the foot of the ladder and called up to the man with my tired old pitch: "Excuse me, sir. I might look like your everyday, street-walkin'…" But my heart wasn't in it. The man looked down and me and said, "No, son. We don't need any pots and pans. Thank you, anyway."

I sighed and turned away. I hadn't gone more than five steps when the man called out from behind me, "By the way, son, what's bothering you?" I stopped short. *How in the world does he know something's bothering me?* I wondered. *I've been faking it pretty well.* And then it hit me—no matter how well I thought I was faking it, I wasn't a good enough actor to hide my lack of confidence. The man on the ladder, and everyone else I'd been pitching, had seen it plain and clear.

I remembered an old proverb from my Sunday school days: *As a man thinketh in his heart, so is he.* When I'd started out, I was successful thanks to a bit of luck and the fact that I didn't know any better. After sales fell off, I could look back on that first week for encouragement. What encouragement did I have now? The circumstances were tragic, but wasn't God, who'd been with me all along, still the same? Maybe I'd been stubborn about telling Him how lost I was and how much I needed Him. I'd never had to say as much, not even in Vietnam. But my faith had never been shaken like this before either. I had always known God was there, but had I really reached out for Him? Maybe I needed to trust that He could help me now, help me close just one deal so I could go on.

I turned around and strode right back to the foot of the ladder. "Hello!" I boomed. "I might look like your everyday, street-walkin', door-bangin' salesman, but I've got the neatest set of pots and pans you ever did see. Could I come in and show 'em to you, please?"

The man looked me straight in the eye and said, "That's more like it, son. Let's take a look." That night Charlie Borland and his wife, Peggy, bought a set of cookware. And I vowed never again to let circumstances control me.

Today, I own Lustre Craft International, the largest distributor of Waterless Cookware by West Bend in the world. Some call it a rags-to-riches story, but I like to call it a journey of faith…because that is precisely what it was. We can't always control what happens to us, but we have power over our reactions to it. God will give us the strength to carry on if we reach out to Him and do things His way.

I've always remembered Charlie Borland for helping me learn that lesson. A few years back I even sent him and his wife a brand-new set of cookware, along with a note that read, *I want to thank you folks. Without you, I might still be breaking rocks in Lick Creek, Illinois.*

$\mathcal{L}$IVING LIFE GOD'S WAY

After reading these true stories of people who experienced God's grace and power in their lives, perhaps you realize that you are at a point in your own life where you need special help from God.

Are you facing a temptation? A broken relationship? A major disappointment?

Are you ready to experience forgiveness and salvation? Encouragement and hope? Wisdom and inspiration? A miracle?

Though God's power and grace are deep and profound, receiving His help is as simple as ABC.

A—Ask: The only place to start is by asking God for help;

B—Believe: You must believe—have faith—that God can help you;

C—Confess: You must confess—admit—that you truly need God's help to receive it.

Living life God's way doesn't mean that all troubles disappear, but it does mean that there will always be Someone to turn to with all your needs. Call on Him now. For more information on how you can live God's way, visit our website at:

www.godswaybooks.com

RIGHTS AND PERMISSIONS

"Home for Christmas" © Gloria Cassity Stargel.

Used by permission. All rights reserved.

"How to Make a Moose Run" © Gary Stanley. From *How to Make a Moose Run*.

Published by Honor Books, a division of Cook Communications Ministries.

Used by permission. All rights reserved.

"I Found Hope" © Kevin Whitworth. Used by permission.

All rights reserved.

"Keep Your Eye on the Ball" © Christy Sterner. Used by permission.

All rights reserved.

"Like a Rock" © Jay Cookingham. Used by permission.

All rights reserved.

"Locking Up for the Night" © Robin Bayne. Used by permission.

All rights reserved.

"No Time to Live" © Gloria Cassity Stargel. Used by permission.

All rights reserved.

"Okay, God, If You're Listening, Why Aren't You Answering?" © Stan Toler.

From *God Has Never Failed Me...* Published by Honor Books,

a division of Cook Communications Ministries.

Used by permission. All rights reserved.

"On Bended Knee" © Carol Termin. Used by permission.

All rights reserved.

"One Summer Day" © Jay Cookingham. Used by permission.

All rights reserved.

"Pinto Beans and Fried Bologna—Now That's a Feast of Faith" © Stan Toler.

From *God Has Never Failed Me...* Published by Honor Books,

a division ofCook Communications Ministries.

Used by permission. All rights reserved.

"Postcards from My Son" © Charlie "Tremendous" Jones. Used by permission.

All rights reserved.

"Redefining Success" © Ed Becker. Used by permission.

All rights reserved.

"Swimming on Daddy's Back" © Gary Stanley. From *How to Make a Moose Run*.

Published by Honor Books, a division of Cook Communications Ministries.

Used by permission. All rights reserved.

$\mathcal{M}$EET THE CONTRIBUTORS

John Ashcroft is the Attorney General of the United States and the former Senator from the state of Missouri.

Ed Becker is a chemical engineer and successful businessman from Canada.

Michael Chang, for many years one of the top tennis players in the world, won the 1989 French Open at the age of 17, becoming the youngest man to ever win a Grand Slam.

Bradley S. Collins is a Substance Abuse and Guidance Counselor who works primarily with at-risk, adolescent and teenaged young men and women in Tulsa, Oklahoma. He also provides services and volunteers at treatment centers and other substance abuse recovery facilities, targeting persons affected by alcoholism and/or other drug additions. Brad has a beautiful teenaged daughter, Whitney, whose spirited presence, insight, and sense of humor provide great motivation for much of his work and writing. Brad can be contacted @ nolesdad@aol.com.

Charles Colson, once a member of Richard M. Nixon's White House team, founded Prison Fellowship Ministries in 1976, after his own stay in prison. The ministry works through the Christian community to mobilize outreach and ministry in response to the needs of prisoners, ex-prisoners, victims, and their families, as well as to advance the application of restorative justice principles within the criminal justice system. Colson is author of *Born Again* and many other best-selling books.

Jay Cookingham, the father of seven children, has been happily married to Christine for 20 years. Although trained as a graphic designer, Jay has been writing poetry, short stories, and articles for as long as he can remember. A featured columnist at *fatherville.com,* he also writes a weekly e-mail newsletter for fathers.

Max Davis draws his insight from a vast and varied background—he has been a collegiate athlete, a truck driver, a coach, a pastor/counselor, and a vacuum cleaner salesman. Max holds degrees in journalism and theology. A master storyteller, he now devotes his time to writing. Max lives with his wife, Alanna, and three children on a farm outside of Baton Rouge, Louisiana.

Billy Diamond, a successful businessman and politician, became Grand Chief of the Cree tribe in northern Quebec, Canada, when he was just 21 years old.

Ken Freeman is author of *Rescued By the Cross: Stepping Out of Your Past and Into God's Purpose.*

Joe Gibbs is one of the most successful coaches in the history of the NFL, most notably during his years as head coach with the Washington Redskins. He led the team to three Super Bowl victories and earned a place in the Pro Football Hall of Fame. Joe now owns a successful NASCAR team.

Nancy B. Gibbs is the author of four books, a weekly religion columnist for two newspapers, a writer for *TWINS* Magazine, and a contributor to numerous books and magazines. Her stories and articles have appeared in seven *Chicken Soup for the Soul* books, *Guideposts* books, *Chocolate for Women, Women's World, Family Circle, Decision, Angels on Earth, On Mission Magazine, Happiness*, and many others. Nancy is a pastor's wife, a mother, and a grandmother. She may be reached at *Daiseydood@aol.com* or by writing to her at P.O. Box 53, Cordele, GA 31010.

Todd and Jedd Hafer have teamed up to writer *Snickers from the Front Pew* and *In the Chatroom With God.* Todd is editorial director for the inspirational book division at Hallmark Cards in Kansas City, Missouri. Jedd is site director The Children's Ark, a home for troubled teens in Colorado Springs, Colorado, and travels the country as a standup comedian.

Paul Henderson's story is based on his winning goal in the 1972 Canada-Russia hockey series, a feat that is still known as the "Goal of the Century."

Charlie "Tremendous" Jones began in the insurance industry at age 22 and built a $100 million business division over the next decade. The author of the classic bestseller, *Life Is Tremendous,* he has spoken to millions of people worldwide over the past 25 years.

Tom Lehman, a professional golfer, was named the PGA player of the year in 1996, after winning the British Open and the PGA Tour Championship. By the following April, he was ranked number one in the world.

Roger Neilson coached in the NHL for 24 years, working with more teams than any man in the history of the game. About 1,400 mourners attended a 90-minute tribute to Neilson at the Northview Pentecostal Church in Peterborough, Ontario, Canada, on Saturday June 28th, 2003. The 69-year-old former NHL coach died on June 21st, after a 3-year battle with cancer.

Kristi Powers is a full time human development specialist—in other words a Mommy! She resides in Wisconsin with her husband Michael and their two young sons, Caleb and Connor. Kristi has been writing stories about her life since she was a little girl, and loves to share her from her heart about her relationship with God.

Michael T. Powers, a youth pastor, resides in Wisconsin with his wife Kristi. His stories appear in sixteen different inspirational books and he is the author of the new book: *HeartTouchers.* For a sneak peek or to join the thousands of world-wide readers on his inspirational e-mail list, visit: *http://www.HeartTouchers.com.* Michael can be reached at: Heart4Teens@aol.com.

Gary Stanley was just 13 when he lost his father—but he still looks back to those memories as the most important (and humorous) lessons on life. He is author of *How to Make a Moose Run* and *What My Dog Has Taught Me About Life.*

Gloria Cassity Stargel is an assignment writer for *GUIDEPOSTS* Magazine; a freelance writer; and author of *The Healing: One Family's Victorious Struggle With Cancer,* published originally by Tyndale House Publishers. *The Healing* has been re-released in special updated edition by Bright Morning Publications. Call 1-800-888-9529 or Visit www.brightmorning.com.

Christy Sterner is the *God's Way* series editorial consultant and has 10 years of experience in the Christian publishing industry. She has written for many series including *Hugs* and *Chicken Soup for the Soul.*

Nanette Thorsen-Snipes is a freelance writer of 20 years and an award-winning author. She began writing in 1981 when her mother was terminally ill with cancer. She began with a year of humorous family columns in a local newspaper. The columns stopped abruptly when her mother died. Though she always had an interest in writing, a strong desire was born at that time to write from her heart.

Stan Toler, an author, a gifted leader, administrator, and inspirational speaker, is known as a "pastor to pastors." In addition to training church leaders throughout North America, Stan serves as the Senior Pastor of *Trinity Church of the Nazarene* in Oklahoma City, Oklahoma http://www.stantoler.com/subpages/menu-items/quick-links/speaking-schedule.shtml.

Joe Tye is creator and producer of *The Twelve Core Action Values,* a comprehensive, systematic curriculum of values-based life and leadership skills. His training programs have helped organizations cultivate a more positive and productive workplace environment. He can be contacted at: joetye@southslope.net

*T*ELL US YOUR STORY

*Can you recall a person's testimony or a time in your own
life when God touched your heart in a profound way?
Would your story encourage others to live God's Way?
Please share your story today, won't you?
God could use it to change a person's life forever.*

For Writer's Guidelines, future titles, and submission
procedures, visit:
www.godswaybooks.com

Or send a postage-paid, self-addressed envelope to:

God's Way Editorial
6528 E. 101st Street, Suite 416
Tulsa, Oklahoma 74133-6754

This and other titles in the God's Way Series
are available from your local bookstore.

God's Way for Fathers
God's Way for Mothers
God's Way for Teens
God's Way for Women

Visit our website at:
www.whitestonebooks.com

*"...To him who overcomes I will give some of the hidden manna to
eat. And I will give him a white stone,
and on the stone a new name written which
no one knows except him who receives it."*
REVELATION 2:17 NKJV

WHITE STONE BOOKS
LAKELAND, FLORIDA